A Guide t
Historically Black Colleges and Universities

This book is a comprehensive, research-based work that brings the best practices and expertise of seminal professionals to the larger Black college environment and beyond. Drawing on data-driven advice from interviews with successful Black college fundraisers and private sector leaders, this book gives practitioners a comprehensive approach for moving away from out-of-date approaches to improve their institutions. Both newcomers and seasoned professionals in the HBCU fundraising arena will benefit from the compelling recommendations offered here.

This practical guide includes:

- **An All Campus Approach**—Discussion goes beyond alumni fundraising strategies to address the blended role that faculty, administrators, and advancement professionals can play to achieve fundraising success.
- **Practical Recommendations**—End-of-chapter suggestions for quick reference, as well as recommendations integrated throughout.
- **Examples of Innovative Approaches**—An entire chapter outlining successful innovative fundraising and engagement programs at various institutions.
- **Extensive Appendices**—Useful resources related to grant procurement, endowments, alumni giving, enrollment and retention, financial aid, and other helpful HBCU information.

Marybeth Gasman is Professor of Higher Education in the Graduate School of Education at the University of Pennsylvania.

Nelson Bowman III is Director of Development at Prairie View A&M University.

"Today and for the foreseeable future, our nation needs HBCUs, and what so many HBCUs need is substantially larger and dependable funds. Applause for Gasman and Bowman for their practical and research-based guide to raising such funds."
— Johnnetta Betsch Cole, President Emerita of Spelman College and Bennett College for Women

"This book is rich with strategies, ideas, and examples. The authors offer clear and practical advice based on solid research to help these critically important institutions build strong, comprehensive, and effective fundraising programs."
— John Lippincott, President of the Council for Advancement and Support of Education

"All stakeholders interested in the financial viability of their institution—development staff, presidents, trustees, alumni, students, and donors—will gain valuable lessons from this book's research-based recommendations that can immediately be applied to their operations."
— Karl W. Reid, Senior Vice President of Academic Programs at UNCF (United Negro College Fund)

A GUIDE TO FUNDRAISING AT HISTORICALLY BLACK COLLEGES AND UNIVERSITIES

AN ALL CAMPUS APPROACH

MARYBETH GASMAN AND NELSON BOWMAN III

Routledge
Taylor & Francis Group

NEW YORK AND LONDON

First published 2012
by Routledge
711 Third Avenue, New York, NY 10017

Simultaneously published in the UK
by Routledge
2 Park Square, Milton Park, Abingdon, Oxon OX14 4RN

Routledge is an imprint of the Taylor & Francis Group, an informa business

© 2012 Taylor & Francis

The right of Marybeth Gasman and Nelson Bowman III to be identified as authors of this work has been asserted by them in accordance with sections 77 and 78 of the Copyright, Designs and Patents Act 1988.

Trademark notice: Product or corporate names may be trademarks or registered trademarks, and are used only for identification and explanation without intent to infringe.

Library of Congress Cataloging in Publication Data
Gasman, Marybeth.
    A guide to fundraising at historically Black colleges and universities :
    an all campus approach / by Marybeth Gasman and Nelson Bowman, III.
    p. cm.
    Includes bibliographical references and index.
    1. African American universities and colleges–Finance. 2. Education,
    Higher–United States–Finance. 3. Educational fund raising–United States.
    I. Bowman, Nelson. II. Title.
    LC2781.G37 2011
    371.2'06–dc23
    2011023766

ISBN: 978–0–415–89272–8 (hbk)
ISBN: 978–0–415–89273–5 (pbk)
ISBN: 978–0–203–81761–2 (ebk)

Typeset in Minion and Scala Sans
by Swales & Willis Ltd, Exeter, Devon

Printed and bound in the United States of America
on acid-free paper by Edwards Brothers, Inc.

SUSTAINABLE FORESTRY INITIATIVE

Certified Fiber Sourcing

www.sfiprogram.org

Dedicated to Charles Stephens—a pioneer in African American philanthropy and HBCU fundraising

CONTENTS

PREFACE

In September of 2008, John S. Wilson, the Executive Director of the White House Initiative on Historically Black Colleges and Universities, stated that the biggest challenge for the nation's Black colleges is fundraising. Specifically, Wilson (2010) said, "Whereas building larger endowments [at HBCUs] is key, there is also an immediate need to build the kind of operational and academic 'scaffolding' required for institutional robustness in areas related and conducive to endowment growth." If Black colleges could meet this challenge they would be much more stable.

In order to ensure success, it is important that we understand what Historically Black Colleges and Universities (HBCUs) are doing in terms of fundraising: What kind of infrastructure exists? Who is involved in fundraising? Black colleges are vitally important not only to the education of African Americans, but to other racial and ethnic minorities as well as low-income students. They are critical to meeting our nation's goals for increased degree attainment and global competitiveness; as such, understanding their fundraising structure and needs is essential.

One of the most important reasons why fundraising success needs to increase at HBCUs is to provide more institutional grant and aid for students. In order to compete for students with majority institutions, which have larger endowments and offer more institutional aid, HBCUs must increase their endowment size (Rust, 2009). To do this, HBCUs have to capitalize on all of their institutional resources and enhance their fundraising ability (Tindall, 2007; Williams & Kritsonis, 2006).

Our book is a comprehensive, research-based text on fundraising within the Black college context. We bring together the best practices and expertise of seminal professionals in the larger Black college environment and beyond. In addition, we aim to persuade Black colleges, which often practice out-of-date approaches and direct their resources into areas that are no longer productive, to change their ways based on our data-driven recommendations.

Much of our data is drawn from interviews with successful Black college fundraisers and others who work within and on behalf of Black colleges (see Appendix B). We also explore practices across Black colleges that are successful and use these to craft a comprehensive approach to fundraising. Lastly, we examine Black colleges that have successfully changed their fundraising practices and we use them as a basis for constructing compelling recommendations for practitioners.

Fundraisers need to be experts at relationship building, managing people, and understanding the academic culture that exists at HBCUs. Both newcomers and seasoned professionals in the HBCU fundraising arena will benefit from this comprehensive book on Black college fundraising. Often fundraisers are faced with uncertainties in their positions. We hope to alleviate these uncertainties by providing expertise, examples, and resources to strengthen fundraisers' understanding of institutional advancement within the HBCU context. We consider the history and traditions of these institutions and provide a rich discussion of the nuances that exist within the HBCU environment.

Unlike other books that have focused solely on alumni fundraising strategies at HBCUs (Gasman & Anderson-Thompkins, 2003), our book presents an "An All Campus Approach," which encompasses the blended role that academics, administrators, and advancement professionals must play to achieve success. We see the various academic and ancillary units, including faculty, student affairs, financial aid, and public relations, as integral to fundraising success. However, we acknowledge that it can be challenging to introduce the idea of fundraising to these traditionally non-fundraising entities (Tindall, 2009). While much of this book focuses on HBCUs, many of the examples and strategies discussed can be used at both majority and other minority serving institutions. We focus on strategies that speak to alumni of color, a population that is quickly increasing at majority institutions, as well as approaches that work within resource-challenged environments.

Especially now, when the future of many Black colleges hangs in the balance, there exists a need for a fundraising book that describes the "circling-the-wagons" of university departments and ancillary units to defend themselves in times of crises. As witnessed throughout our nation's history, communities of color, whether trying to preserve their culture or their organizations, have had to look inward and recognize untapped internal strengths. Through self-assessment, it is possible to identify areas of ineffectiveness and inefficiency—areas in which capitalizing on our human and financial strengths are greatly needed. Priorities sometimes need to be modified to better speak to a changing economic or political climate as the stakes are high and getting higher. Traditionally, HBCUs have claimed to do "more with less," but if an all campus approach is adopted in full, these institutions will increase their fundraising success and finally, in the words of the former Spelman and Bennett College Johnnetta B. Cole, be able to "do more with more."

THE IMPORTANCE OF HBCUs

Although those in the HBCU community understand the importance of these historic institutions, oftentimes outsiders do not. In addition, sometimes even insiders are not aware of the strengths and accomplishments of HBCUs as a whole. Knowing these strengths is not only an important justification for a book on HBCU fundraising, but it is essential material to have when cultivating and soliciting donors. First and foremost, students at HBCUs feel a "strong desire for a sense of belonging." In particular, students want access to an intimate cultural environment that welcomes them. They also want to be a part of college campus that empowers them both culturally and academically (Awokoya & Mann, 2011). Research, most recently that of Terrell L. Strayhorn (2009) shows that a "sense of belonging" is absolutely instrumental to the success of students—especially students of color. HBCUs provide this sense of belonging. HBCU students also want to grow intellectually in an environment "devoid of racism" and that celebrates African American cultural heritage (Awokoya & Mann, 2011). Research shows that having a deep sense of one's culture, especially the positive contributions of others like you, plays a significant role in academic success (Freeman & Cohen, 2001).

According to a recent report issued by the United States Commission on Civil Rights (2010), HBCUs have considerable strengths. First and foremost, students without optimal academic credentials are much more likely to succeed at an HBCU because of the supportive environment. HBCUs boast an environment in which students are more engaged, both socially and academically, than their counterparts on majority campuses. Given lower funding levels and the underprepared nature of some students, HBCUs are "doing a much better job" than majority institutions at educating African American students. One of the main reasons for the success of HBCU students is their close relationships with faculty members. Faculty members' dedication to teaching, student-support networks, encouragement to pursue leadership posts in their fields of study, and the availability and access of faculty role models help to explain the success of an HBCU education—both empirically and anecdotally. In fact, HBCU students are 1.5 times more likely than their counterparts at Historically White Institutions (HWIs) to collaborate with a faculty member on a research project (United States Commission on Civil Rights, 2010). According to a recent report issued by the United Negro College Fund's Frederick D. Patterson Research Institute (Awokoya & Mann, 2011), students at HBCUs had consistent and meaningful interactions with faculty members who looked like them and often had similar backgrounds. In addition, students felt that the professors went "beyond their professionally related responsibilities by expressing genuine interest and concern for their students' entire development." Research confirms that having faculty role models leads to success for students of color. Moreover, researchers have found that HBCU faculty members often provide a holistic approach to student learning, engaging students in their development both academically and personally (Palmer & Gasman, 2008).

Another strength of HBCUs is in the production of graduate and professional students. Of the top 21 undergraduate producers of African American science Ph.D.s, 17 were HBCUs. Of note, many of those students would have been considered underprepared by majority institutions. And, although HBCU students tend to have lower SAT scores and high-school grades than their African-American counterparts at many majority institutions, HBCUs produce 40 percent of Black science and engineering degrees with only 20 percent of Black enrollment (Perna et al., 2009).

HBCUs also produce students who care about their surrounding communities and give back professionally and personally. For example, nearly half of the nation's African-American teachers graduated from HBCUs. Unfortunately, this fact is rarely acknowledged by the media or policymakers. Moreover, HBCU students are more likely to give to charity and to be more politically active. They are also more likely to participate in service learning and religious activities.

Despite facing many challenges in the 21st Century, HBCUs have considerable strengths that should be highlighted within and beyond the HBCU community. Imagine if majority institutions used the strategies employed by HBCUs to educate African Americans and other students of color. Students would have much richer educational experiences. Too often, researchers and policymakers only think about the ways that HBCUs can learn from majority schools, forgetting that these historic institutions have much to teach us about educating Black and low-income students.

OVERVIEW OF CHAPTERS

The book is laid out in eleven chapters that focus on the various aspects of fundraising within the HBCU community. Chapter 1, entitled "Taking Inventory," gives practitioners the tools to assess their fundraising program and draw some conclusions with regard to what they need to move forward and improve. Chapter 2, "The Role of the President," examines the engagement of the HBCU college president in fundraising. We discuss the need for the president to understand the college's fundraising goals and how these goals connect to the institution's strategic plan. This chapter incorporates the wisdom of presidents who have successfully engaged their development staffs as well as commentary from development officers who have productive relationships with their presidents. In addition, we discuss one of the most important tasks the president has in terms of his or her fundraising roll—that of engaging the institution's board of trustees.

In Chapter 3, "Academic Deans, Faculty, and Student Services Involvement," which focuses on involving academic deans, faculty, and student services staff outside of advancement in the fundraising process of the institution, we discuss the ways in which these internal constituents can be engaged and shown the importance of their role. In particular, we examine the part that deans can play in encouraging faculty involvement in fundraising as well as the key role that student affairs and student services practitioners play in both facilitating giving and hindering it.

Chapter 4, titled "Alumni Giving and Engagement," urges readers to define who their alumni are and assess the quality of the relationship these alumni have with their institution. We discuss the importance of alumni engagement and giving, including annual giving, to the future success of an institution. Moreover, this chapter explores the often-volatile relationships between HBCUs and their alumni associations, providing insight into how to make these relationships stronger and more productive. Lastly, the chapter examines the role of student advancement and alumni groups in creating future alumni.

In Chapter 5, "Engaging Affinity Groups," we discuss the various affinity groups at HBCUs, including classes, fraternities, sororities, social service organizations, and student leaders. We also describe ways of engaging these affinity groups to more effectively support the institution. Many of these affinity groups have life long affiliations, which emphasize service and giving back. HBCUs need to tap into the strength and loyalty of these organizations.

Throughout their history HBCUs have benefitted from corporate and foundation support, albeit not at the same levels as their historically White counterparts. Within the hostile environment of the segregated South, many HBCUs came to see this type of support as a saving grace. In Chapter 6, "Corporate and Foundation Giving," we encourage HBCU practitioners to engage corporations and foundations for support while simultaneously securing donations from alumni and other private donors. Moreover, we examine the motivations behind corporation and foundation support of HBCUs.

Endowments at HBCUs are comparatively low as there has not been a long-term focus on building them. Without a robust financial endowment, it is nearly impossible to be innovative and create new programs to sustain the institution. Chapter 7, "Building Endowments," focuses on strengthening both the mechanisms behind endowments as well as strategies to enhance their value.

HBCUs often forget to tell their own story. When they miss an opportunity to show the many successes they've had in spite of the hardships they face, they cede control of their image to often hostile outside forces. As a result, most of the media coverage of HBCUs is negative. Chapter 8, "Telling a Better Story," examines successful publicity stories and their impact on fundraising. As most HBCUs have little funding for publicity, we discuss low-cost, high-impact ways to bolster the image of an institution.

Chapter 9, "Innovative Fundraising and Engagement Programs," highlights several innovative approaches HBCUs are using to increase financial support and garner greater affinity to their institutions. In Chapter 10, "Background on Historically Black Colleges and Universities," we provide a historical backdrop on HBCUs for those who are interested in the topic of fundraising, but perhaps are not as well acquainted with the HBCU context. And, lastly, the concluding chapter, "Concluding Thoughts," makes recommendations for improving fundraising at HBCUs and offers general insights on how they can be financially successful and meet future challenges.

We want this book to be as helpful and practical as possible so we have also included appendices related to grant procurement, endowments, alumni giving, enrollment and retention, financial aid, and other helpful HBCU information. In addition, we have included our interview questions.

Lastly, it is important to note what this book is not. It is not a fundraising 101 book. We assume that readers will have a general knowledge of fundraising and the various components. What we offer is an approach to fundraising that will enhance HBCUs and other under resourced institutions that need to be innovative and creative.

ACKNOWLEDGMENTS

It took a lot of blood, sweat, and tears to get to where we are today, but we have just begun. Today we begin the earnest work of making sure the world we leave our children is just a little better than the one we inhabit today.

Barack H. Obama

I found that among its other benefits, giving liberates the soul of the giver.

Maya Angelou

Writing a book is a rewarding yet arduous task. In writing this one, we were lucky to draw upon the expertise of many of those in institutional advancement at the nation's Historically Black Colleges and Universities (HBCUs). These individuals, who are featured in the book, were gracious with their time and sharing of expertise. We are also thankful to the college presidents that talked with us, sharing their strategies for successful fundraising and the elevation of their institutions. They were both inspiring and informative.

In researching this book, we also benefitted from the research of others who have spent time examining the strengths and challenges of HBCUs as well as the profession of fundraising. Both areas of study are fairly young and we hope that our work will inspire others to do more research in these areas—especially research that focuses on fundraising in minority serving institutions and among people of color.

We are particularly grateful to two research assistants who helped with this project. First, Jessica Elmore, who currently serves as the Assistant Director of Multicultural Alumni Programs at Kansas State University, helped us to prepare the chapter on innovative fundraising programs at HBCUs. She scoured the Internet for the most interesting programs—especially those that could be easily replicated. Second, Thai-Huy Nguyen helped us immensely by gathering articles and books, setting up interviews, securing permissions, creating the appendices, and just being damn efficient! Thanks Jessica and Thai! Both of these young scholars have wonderful careers ahead of them. We wish them well.

We are grateful to our families for supporting us during the research and writing process of the book. In particular, we'd like to thank Michelle, Edward, Lilly, Nelse (PaPa), Chloe, and Kyle for their love, patience, and joy.

Lastly, although we may appear to be an unlikely co-author team, it has been a joy to work together. We share a love of laughing and this made the writing sessions just a little easier. Not only was the writing fun, but we explored a topic about which we both feel very passionate—HBCUs. And, although we are sometimes critical of HBCUs in this book, our critique is rooted in a desire to see HBCUs improve and thrive. We hope you enjoy *A Guide to Fundraising at Historically Black Colleges and Universities* and that it helps you in your quest to support HBCUs.

Marybeth Gasman, Philadelphia, PA
Nelson Bowman III, Houston, TX

1

TAKING INVENTORY

Anyone working within the area of institutional advancement would enjoy having a ready-made, fully-resourced operation. However, at many Historically Black Colleges and Universities (HBCUs), having only a partially complete fundraising infrastructure is often the norm. In some cases, advancement offices may consist of as few as three people—a director, a secretary, and a do-everything-else person (Gasman & Anderson-Thompkins, 2003). Possessing only the bare essentials, these small shops often accomplish great feats. It would be ideal to have a full fundraising staff, including key personnel such as major gift officers, a planned giving team, a prospect researcher, a grant writer, and an annual fund department. Given the success of some HBCUs with mere skeleton staffs, imagine what they could achive with full-scale resources (Gasman & Anderson-Thompkins, 2003). Moreover, with additional funds, HBCUs could provide much needed education, professional training, and technical assistance to their staffs. In the interim, however, HBCUs need to capitalize on the resources that they do have. In this chapter, we suggest ways for HBCUs, and their advancement offices, in particular, to take an inventory of their resources. Doing so will help make the rest of this book more useful and provide a road map for what is possible in terms of fundraising.

Oftentimes HBCUs need to be creative in their use of resources. The idea of going to the administration and requesting additional funding, historically and during these current economic times, has never proven to be effective—there just is not extra money. In doing research for this book, we spent a considerable amount of time speaking with development professionals at HBCUs, but also at historically White institutions. What we found is that majority institutions do not always have unlimited resources either. The fact that now many majority institutions have million dollar plus annual budgets and advancement staffs that number in the hundreds is more of a testament to these institutions initiating a formalized development approach, decades and, in some cases, centuries ago (coupled with their alumni's access to wealth). "It takes time, commitment and a few successes to build a complete advancement staff made up of all the trimmings. Everyone at the intuition must be on the same page, recognizing the commitment and re-investment required to sustain and enhance a top-notch advancement area," said one vice president of advancement of a majority institution. She went on to mention that upon accepting the position 10 years ago, there was only a 20-person development staff, doing their best to work with a paltry $750,000 budget. However, through establishing a plan for growth along with the university's support (non-financial), she was able to virtually triple the resources of her department. Admittedly, her initial small staff and budget more than triples the current make-up of most HBCU shops. However, the point to her message is that we must invest in institutional advancement and build upon it in order to enhance its capacity and thus, enhance the institution as a whole.

MAXIMIZING STAFF

There is no such thing as a ready-made fundraising shop and most HBCUs can still remember the time when the development office was simply a "catch-all bucket" for whatever might fall in as there were few organized or formal development initiatives. The most important way to begin is to assess your current inventory of resources and determine if certain modifications can garner better results. For example, at one HBCU, the chief development officer decided that there was a need for more front-line development officers to cultivate a newly-identified donor base. As a result of the institution's first phon-a-thon, the development office discovered over 200 new donors. Together, these donors had a giving capacity in excess of $6 million. With a goal of increasing the university's alumni giving rate from a single to double digit, the chief development officer decided to focus a substantial portion of the department's attention and resources on this untapped constituency.

As there were no funds available to hire additional personnel to solicit the new donors, the development leadership asked existing staff members to expand their current roles and assume additional responsibilities. Staff members were asked if they wanted to move into front-line development positions. Overwhelmingly, the answer was yes as everyone saw this as an opportunity to move up within the institution and to expand their skills, thereby increasing their value to the HBCU. An added benefit to expanding the positions of staff members is greater engagement on the part of the advancement employees. They take on more ownership of the HBCU and this ownership leads to an increased commitment to their position and a desire for more responsibility.

Of course, it is great to add more front-line fundraisers, but they are of no help and actually could cause the HBCU embarrassment if they are not properly trained. One inexpensive, yet effective way to train advancement staff members is for the senior development staff to conduct in-house trainings. These more experienced fundraisers can provide "Fundraising 101" sessions that include a basic understanding of fundraising principles and strategies. Oftentimes, more senior fundraisers have attended sessions hosted by the Council for the Advancement and Support of Education (CASE) or the Association of Fundraising Professionals (AFP) and can use their acquired knowledge to craft training sessions for other staff members.

ASSESSING RELATIONSHIPS ON CAMPUS

In order to maximize fundraising potential, the office of advancement needs to have positive and productive relationships across campus. It is important to reach out to academic deans as well as student service-oriented offices. In many cases, these relationships are not in place and those on the academic side of the house and in customer service act as if they are in silos rather than seeing how they complement the overall mission of the institution. Because those in advancement are in the position of bringing external constituents to the campus, they have a vantage point that allows them to see the bigger picture. They understand the importance of unity on campus and how essential this unity is to potential donors.

DATABASE MANAGEMENT AND CLEANING

What type of database does your advancement office use? Is it an Excel spreadsheet or an actual database management system such as Razors Edge? Most institutions of higher education use some sophisticated system for storing, managing, and retrieving information related to the finance department, financial aid, and student records. However, we were surprised to learn that many HBCUs are not using the alumni and development components of the database software. While several reasons were given for the lack of use, the most common was cost of the additional software components. It is important to note here that it takes money to make money. And as with any process, investing in automation increases proficiency and saves time.

Another important tool to enhancing fundraising is a prospect research instrument such as Wealth Engine. While the search engine Google has provided the average computer user faster searching capacity than ever thought possible, it poses nowhere near the capabilities of many of the of the wealth identification programs that are now available. Being able to access critical financial and biographical information about your prospects in a quick and efficient manner is essential to honing in on those potential donors with the greatest giving capacity.

Knowing your alumni means more than just knowing their names and graduation years. The real question lies in the reliability of your data. Are you able to successfully contact them via phone, mail, and email? Maintaining accurate data is often a major challenge for HBCUs as, in most cases, this regimine has not been sustained throughout the institution's existence. According to a report on alumni giving by Ayers & Associates (2002), "the percent of addressable alumni is slightly lower at HBCUs" compared to majority institutions (p. 5). This lack of efficiency usually means a very expensive data cleansing will be necessary in order to achieve the desired effect—clean alumni records. In many cases, data scrubs can cost upwards of $20,000 depending on the number of records and this causes many HBCUs to be somewhat reluctant to invest in the service. Admittedly, data cleansing is a costly expenditure, one that may require a higher level administrative decision, but what is the alternative? Basically, the institution continues to send out communication and solicitation pieces that are returned unde-liverable, wasting precious resources. However, if the institu-tion's goal is reaching more of its main constituency and increas-ing its alumni giving rates, data cleansing is the foundation for such goals.

One director of development at an HBCU told us a story of having a century of alumni data records that had never been thoroughly cleaned. For years, the advancement office had rec-ommended the need for investing in itself only to be met with strong opposition for such a large expenditure as data cleansing. Finally, following a direct mailing in which 25 percent of the out-going pieces were returned, the administration agreed that something had to be done to improve the delivery rate of future mailings. As a result of the data cleanse, the HBCU was able to update 57 percent of alumni addresses and 76 percent of alumni phone numbers. Moreover, it was able to add 20 percent more alumni emails.

HBCUs need to work hard to communicate with more alumni through electronic means as the world is moving toward mostly electronic forms of communication. With email, communica-tion is basically instant and recipients can read their mail any-where. Having access to the emails of alumni allows the HBCU to reach both larger and small audiences at roughly the same cost, and little cost for that matter. This is especially impor-tant as educational fundraising budgets are becoming smaller and smaller. Also, of note, email messages can be altered and segmented to appeal to specific audiences in relatively simple ways. Compared to printing costs, email communication is highly efficient. Despite these advantages, HBCUs need to remember that many of their alumni are nostalgic and the leg-acy of the institution may not be conveyed through email. Email is not personal and when you are trying to convey a sense of warmth it is not always effective. In addition, a large percentage of the alumni at HBCUs is older and tends to like to feel and touch communication from their alma mater. Knowing how people prefer to be communicated with is essential to fundraising success. Surveying alumni can lead to more information on their needs and preferences.

IDENTIFYING POTENTIAL DONORS

In addition to updating data on alumni, it is essential to identify non-alumni donors as well. To ascertain who these donors are requires a considerable amount of research. One of the best resources for identifying potential donors is the Foundation Center, which hosts a database of foundations and their specific funding interests. However, before approaching a foundation or corporation for support, it is essential to do an internal audit of unmet campus needs.

One way to identify unmet needs is to poll the various campus units and ask for a list of programs and initiatives that they would like to fund but that are not part of the annual budget. Ascertaining these unmet needs is important as it allows the institution to approach foundations and corporations with its own ideas rather than merely reacting to requests for proposals or foundation-led initiatives. For example, at Prairie View A&M University, the administrators at the College of Nursing recognized that very few students were interested in pursuing Ph.D.s in nursing with the goal of becoming faculty. They also realized that most of their faculty members were White and as a result students did not see pursuing a Ph.D. as being a viable career option due to the lack of African American role models. According to the 2009 American Association of Colleges of Nurses member schools data, only 11.6 percent of full-time nursing faculty comes from minority backgrounds, and in Texas the numbers are even less diverse. Overall, there continues to be an under-representation of non-Caucasian groups in the nursing faculty workforce. These low numbers can have a negative effect on students enrolled in nursing programs in that students are not prepared to provide culturally sensitive care for the ethnically diverse city of Houston and the state's population (Texas Department of State Health Services Center, 2006).

Over the past 93 years and more specifically since 1970, the Prairie View College of Nursing has proven to be a model of success with its broadened admissions, enrollment, and graduation of a multicultural undergraduate and graduate student body comprised of Whites, Asians, Hispanics, and international students. Along with this proven track record and the growing nursing shortage, estimated to be 20,000 by 2013, the Prairie View advancement team in conjunction with the College of Nursing approached the Houston Endowment, Inc. with a strategy to remove the barriers to access, which continue to exist in Texas for under-represented minority students being enrolled in a Ph.D. nursing program. Most importantly, the aim was to increase the diversity in the Ph.D. educational pipeline and have a positive effect on the nursing workforce for Houston. Convinced that this was a good idea, the foundation awarded Prairie View $3 million to support the Ph.D. program initiative.

Another example of identifying unmet needs can be found at Philander Smith College. When President Walter Kimbrough secured the leadership position at the institution, he noticed that the small college did not have an institutional niche. Although the institution had been in the Little Rock, Arkansas area for years, many locals could not identify its strengths. Having a deep regard for social justice at all levels, Kimbrough worked with faculty, staff, and students to revamp the College's mission, resulting in a purposeful focus on social justice. The new mission is aptly titled "Think Justice." In order to amplify this new mission and solidify it with local and national communities, Philander Smith approached the Kresge Foundation. Kimbrough, along with the advancement team, made a connection between social justice, service learning, and civic engagement for the foundation. He made it clear that Philander Smith students would do more than build their own careers—they would reach out to the communities around them, giving back and uplifting those in need. With this effort, Kimbrough met student and community needs while simultaneously creating an innovative and fresh approach to education. He made his institution stand apart from others.

Creating an institutional niche is an important strategy for securing external support for an HBCU. If you cannot communicate what your institution is good at and what it is known for, it is nearly impossible for others, including funders, to recognize institutional strengths. It is important that HBCUs do not try to be everything to everyone but instead that they play to their institutional strengths. If HBCUs develop excellent programs, they can tout the success and importance of these programs and avoid conversations about weaker programs. When interacting with the media or donors, HBCU presidents and development officers need to be able to recall their institutional strengths immediately.

WAYS OF STEWARDING DONORS

How often does your advancement office say thank you to donors? What are the various methods used to show appreciation? Research indicates that donors should be stewarded a minimum of seven times per gift. By definition, stewardship is the careful and responsible management of something entrusted to one's care. As such, within the fundraising context, this "something" is the donor and the management refers to the way in which the donor is engaged by the HBCU following a gift to the institution. Stewardship begins with the acknowledgment of the gift in written form. From that point, the idea is to show continued appreciation in a multitude of ways. For instance, donors should be included in special events on campus, asked to serve on institutional committees, invited to speak to students about their areas of expertise, and updated on the use of their gift.

CHIEF ADVANCEMENT OFFICER

As the chief advancement officer, there are a number of things that need to be in place or coming into place in order to be a successful fundraiser. Assuming that many of you may be first generation development officers, having never solicited for a nonprofit, be aware that there are some similarities between development and the corporate world. However, there are several differences and you need to know them.

Many development officers come from a corporate management and sales background, possessing the ability to convince others to see things their way—with that said, they never doubt their ability to persuade potential donors to invest in the university. However, the thing that is so incredibly different between the corporate and the academic world is the foundation on which each is based.

In the corporate world, the number of products or services sold tends to be the only barometer that matters. In the academic world, it is about the quality of the institution's educational programs, which is measured by increased retention and graduation rates of students. Academic programs, unlike corporate products, are intangibles that cannot be counted or inventoried and, in many cases, are extremely difficult to explain in layperson's terms. Realizing and internalizing these differences is key as consumers and donors can be one and the same, but their views and expectation are distinctly different.

As a new development officer to an HBCU institution, especially someone coming from another industry, you must take time to gain an understanding of higher education and how those (academicians) that live in that world view it. One should begin by learning the history of the institution through reading various materials such as historical pieces written by those associated and not associated with the university. The idea here is to ascertain balanced information on the institution's accomplishments and struggles. Also, seek out faculty and staff members that have been around for the past quarter-century or more as they will often fill in the blanks with information that was never recorded. Think of them as the wise elders of the town or village that have usually worked through several administrations—many will let you know, *"I was here before the president got here and I'll be here after they are gone."*

The next thing to do is visit each college and school on the campus to gain a better grasp of the unique educational opportunities your institution has to offer in addition to understanding unmet needs. If possible, start at the top by meeting with deans and department heads. However, as a newcomer to campus, such high level access may take some time. Senior faculty and administrative assistants will make for good fill-ins until access is granted to those at the top.

Once armed with information on where help is needed, develop a few strategies for securing external support. Start by researching funding opportunities that match unmet needs that are no longer or have never been funded by the institution's annual budget. From there, create a cultivation plan for obtaining support and offer to share it with deans. A plan well thought-out will usually get the deans' attention and your foot in the door. This will also often lead to regular interactions as now the deans will view you as someone who has their areas' interest at heart.

As the development officer, the assumption is that you are the consummate communicator and relationship builder—you bring people together so that both sides can benefit from each other. The idea of reaching across the aisle to cultivate relationships with deans is the same approach you would attempt with potential donors that may be interested in your institution.

USING THE RESOURCES THAT YOU HAVE

In most HBCU development shops, there is never an overabundance of resources but rather smaller morsels of essentials. This long-standing tradition of having to "do more with less" is certainly not new to Black colleges as they have always suffered disproportionately in terms of infrastructure resources. Another reason for this lack of resources is the difference in the level of attention given to private sector fundraising constituencies. While there is evidence that supports the theory—steady cultivation of alumni will lead to increased giving rates—the idea of doing away with long-standing traditions like only seeking governmental funding is not always well-received. This is especially true among public HBCUs as the formalized fundraising structure at these institutions in still relatively new, comparatively speaking.

Sometimes a decision to realign the focus or, in some extreme cases, making a choice to discontinue an academic area that no longer generates interest allows for the re-allocation of existing resources for a better use. For example, at Spelman College, President Beverly Tatum restructured the institution's curriculum. The institution eliminated its formal education department, which included four programs (child development, secondary teacher certification, pre-school certification, and child development). Those Spelman students interested in teaching can now pursue this degree through the educational students program, an umbrella program for education-related curriculum offerings. Although anchored at Spelman, the program capitalizes on the strengths of nearby HBCUs Morehouse and Clark Atlanta, which offer many education-related courses in their curriculum. Spelman students are able to take classes at either of these institutions (National Public Radio, 2009).

In addition to re-allocating resources, HBCUs need to be very creative in their use of the existing resources available to them. There are many fundraising training programs available at a relatively low cost. For example, the Association of Fundraising Professionals offers one-day educational conferences that are tailored to meet the needs of new and emerging fundraisers and volunteers. These conferences, often titled "Ask the Experts," include a plenary session as well as concurrent sessions. Session topics range from annual giving to career development to ethics and are facilitated by seasoned fundraisers. Because the registration fees for these events are relatively low, HBCUs can send multiple people or sometimes their entire advancement team to them. The most efficient approach to attending this kind of conference is to "canvas the conference" or make sure that the advancement staff attend different sessions, covering as much ground as possible, and taking notes that can later be presented to the rest of the team.

Another inexpensive, yet highly effective, way of training staff and maximizing resources is participation in the webinars offered by the AFP and the CASE. Webinars are convenient and allow you to bring training directly to your campus. They also allow many staff members to learn for the price of one individual.

Taking an inventory of the advancement office is the first step to enhancing the HBCUs' fundraising capabilities. A comprehensive review of all areas, including staff, relationships, and technology is vital to moving to a new level.

Practical Recommendations

- Offer administrative staff members new opportunities that include fundraising in order to strengthen the breadth and skills of your development office.
- Determine your unmet needs throughout the campus so that they will be readily identifiable when working with both donors and private funders.
- Assess your cross-campus relationships and determine

how these relationships can potentially benefit donor cultivation and fundraising efforts.

- Invest in database software to enhance your institution's fundraising ability and efficiency.
- Consider cleansing your institution's data to enhance your fundraising ability and effectiveness in terms of donor outreach and communication.
- Examine your institution's ways of communicating with alumni and donors, determining if these ways are the most beneficial and effective.
- Consider the ways your institution stewards donors and whether or not these methods are effective.

2

THE ROLE OF THE PRESIDENT

I think of myself as the chief fundraiser for the college and my principle responsibility is to tell the story of the school and invite investors to consider Morehouse.

Robert Franklin, Morehouse College President

Today's president must become a strategic thinker and leader. Both of these roles justify the need for presidents to spend a high percentage of their time on the economic health of their institutions.

Changing the Odds, 2005

As the ultimate leader of the institution, college and university presidents must be involved, supportive, and understanding of the institution's fundraising goals (Hodson, 2010). In addition, they must be able to articulate that goal in connection to the institution's mission and strategic plan. The college president is the living logo of any college or university. Moreover, the only way for an organization to realize its full potential is if the president is willing to devote a great deal of his or her time—much of it off campus—to developing and sustaining these relations. Research shows the most effective college and university presidents are the champions of their institution (Eldredge, 1999; Whitaker, 2005). They inspire donor confidence (Fischer, 1985; Hodson, 2010). Presidents must seek capable and influential community leaders to be members of the board of trustees. Likewise, a president needs to be highly visible, participating in boards of both nonprofits and for profits. These types of activities lead to more visibility for his or her institution and identify possibilities for mutual action between the college and key constituencies. The success of the fundraising program falls on the president. In this chapter, we lay out the many roles of the president in the fundraising process, drawing on the literature, our own expertise, and the advice of highly successful HBCU presidents and their chief development officers.

CENTRALITY OF FUNDRAISING TO THE PRESIDENTIAL ROLE

In this day and age, fundraising is an integral part of the president's role. It is not an extra-curricular activity. According to Hodson (2010), the president should give fundraising the same status and priority as other parts of the job. "Rather than being viewed as an isolated or 'special' activity, fundraising should be seen by the president as part of his or her role to securing financing for the institution" (p. 40). Presidents need to spend time on this aspect of their role on a daily basis rather than on an ad hoc basis. They need to be available to the advancement staff regularly, with bi-monthly meetings aimed at being aware of and up-to-date on all major prospects. Presidents can be most effective in their fundraising role if they learn to listen and trust the advice and recommendations of their advancement staff.

Likewise, advancement staff members are more likely to feel confident about their role and in fact, empowered to do their job if the president pays attention to it. The president plays an essential role in inspiring and empowering those within the institution to participate in raising funds to sustain the college or university (Hodson, 2010).

A president who showcases an ideal relationship with his advancement staff, in terms of interaction and communication, is Robert Franklin of Morehouse College. According to Franklin, "The Vice President and I set aside Mondays for management meetings." As a result of these meetings, which also include other advancement staff members, Franklin is continually up-to-date on the major prospects. He is prepared to meet with them and make an "ask" if necessary at any point. Franklin estimates that he spends at least half of his time on fundraising and this shows in terms of Morehouse College's performance. In Franklin's words, "I would say certainly half of my time [is spent on fundraising]. It varies but the average would be half the week, I'm doing something. I'm spending time with my board—conferring with them, educating, cajoling them." This is particularly important at HBCUs where the formalized fundraising process is still relatively new, comparatively speaking. As faculty and staff throughout the institution witness upper level administrators engaging in fundraising, they will feel more comfortable contributing as well.

One of the keys to success in fundraising within the HBCU context is a positive, open relationship between the president and the vice president of advancement. Walter Kimbrough, president of Philander Smith College, is purposeful about his interactions with Shannon Fleming, his vice president of advancement. In Kimbrough's words, "We meet twice a month. Shannon sits with me and gives me updates on donors as well as special projects. We have strategy sessions. We do a lot of cultivating together—getting people to campus and letting them talk to students and faculty." The close relationship, involving constant discussions about potential donors and continual idea generation that Kimbrough has with his vice president is essential to increasing fundraising potential at the large donor level. Large donors need to be continually stewarded and having a consistent strategy to provide this stewarding makes this possible.

Successful presidents in the area of fundraising focus on strategy (Hodson, 2010; Tindall, 2009). Resources within the HBCU context are often scarce and, as such, there can be competition for them among the different entities of the institution. The president must be "responsible for determining the institution's most significant financial needs" and academic priorities (Hodson, 2010; Barrett, 2006). The fundraising strategy should align with the institution's strategic plan. However, it should not exceed reality nor set the fundraising team up for failure (Hodson, 2010). A fundraising strategy should be realistic and tied to the strengths of the institution and the fundraising staff. The fundraising team needs to provide feedback on institutional strategy and they can help determine what is feasible in terms of funding and potential donors. For example, Charlie Nelms at North Carolina Central University meets with his advancement staff on a monthly basis to discuss strategies for soliciting donors as well as new prospects. Likewise, Jim Anderson, the chancellor of Fayetteville State University meets with his vice chancellor, Arthur Affleck, and his staff on a regular basis. The meetings are focused on identifying potential targets for fundraising and strategies for approaching these targets.

Affleck relayed a great strategy for identifying potential donors; he learned it when working with Johnnetta B. Cole at Bennett College for Women. President Cole, who often traveled on behalf of the institution and the many boards on which she served, would return to campus with business cards after every trip. According to Affleck, "She would come back and she was always thinking in fundraising mode when we met. We would then strategize about the individuals. I always had new leads because she was always in fundraising mode." When working with a new president, James Anderson, Affleck encouraged him to use Cole's approach to increasing the potential donor pool. He asked his president, "What meetings do you have planned, where are you going, where have you been so that I can have you thinking about potential donors wherever you go?"

An essential aspect of supporting the fundraising arm of the institution as president is a willingness to travel and interact with alumni in official campus-sponsored events as well as in individual meetings. As the president is the leader of the institution both in practice and symbolically, alumni and donors want to interact with this individual in meaningful ways. According to Hodson (2010), "the president should remember that there are times when the only reason he [or she] is in the room is because he [or she] is a living embodiment of the university" (p. 42). At Prairie View A&M University, President George C. Wright often participates in "awareness gatherings." These gatherings are an opportunity for the president to speak candidly about the current state of the institution in an intimate setting. Basically, the conversation is special and focuses on information that is not readily available in a newsletter. Of note, these awareness gatherings are often held in an alumnus's home so that both the president and the alumni feel comfortable and relaxed during the exchange. This environment allows the alumni to become reacquainted with the institution. Prior to the event, the development office gathers information on the guest list, including background and wealth screenings. This preparation enables the fundraising officers and president to identify key prospects who should receive extra attention from the president.

While interaction with all graduates is vitally important, during these "awareness gatherings," which are much like "fire-side chats," it is important that the president maximize the time to interact with high level prospects. In the words of Charlie Nelms, "every prospect is important, but not every prospect is of equal importance." As HBCUs have limited resources, they need to focus their efforts on cultivating high level donors, while simultaneously maintaining strong relationships with those smaller donors who give consistently. Presidents, in particular, need to "keep in mind that donors view their gift not as a donation but as an investment in the institution" (Hodson, 2010: 34).

Presidents need to establish a balance when it comes to fundraising and the amount of time they spend in the area. According to Charlie Nelms, "I'm extremely accessible, extremely accessible. Sometimes I worry that I may be too accessible. What I have found at my HBCU, I won't generalize about them all, is that there's a tendency sometimes for people to want to deal directly with the president or the chancellor in my case. So respect for the chain of command among alumni compared to when I was at majority institution [is not always there]. At the majority institutions where I worked, people did not feel slighted if my advancement person did all of the arrangements and worked with them up to a certain point. But here I have found that there has been this kind of premature engagement in many instances of the chancellor … it is what it is and so you take it and you try to [shape it] into what you think it needs to be." According to researchers, fundraising staff members need to be respectful of a president's time and only include him or her if the president's presence adds great value (Hodson, 2010; Barrett, 2006).

The amount of access that a president gives all donors is contingent on the institution's fundraising situation, meaning how much fundraising success the college or university has had and is experiencing. The circumstances under which a president leads make a difference. For example, President Franklin at Morehouse College, which is one of the most successful HBCUs in the fundraising area, is more restrictive in terms of whom he interacts with among donors. His time is limited and he tends to restrict high level interaction to wealthier individuals. According to Franklin, "Associate vice presidents focus on the leadership gifts, so $50,000 and over, with more of a concentration on the $100,000 plus donors. And, then the vice president and I work in a more targeted way with seven figure and above prospects."

On the opposite end of the spectrum is Michael Sorrell who leads a struggling, yet highly innovative, small college in Dallas, Texas—Paul Quinn College. In Sorrell's words, "I'm accessible to everyone. I believe very much that if we are charting a new course for an institution the best voice for that is mine. I don't want to be like the incredible Oz behind the curtain." Because of the institution's more recent financial struggles, Sorrell has had to take on the role of chief development officer himself—hoping to hire someone in the near future. Sorrell describes his experience:

> When I came in as president, we had a fundraising office and it was pretty ineffective. So I kept trying to hire people and nobody wanted to come and raise money for Paul Quinn College. So then I started thinking if we can't get experienced fundraisers, can we take smart people who are organized and teach them to be fundraisers? So we tried that and then we brought in someone who had experience in fundraising at a majority institution to manage that staff and that was a disaster. If you are someone who has only raised money in what I would call a "milk and cookies environment" [where all the resources are in place, working efficiently] this one is going to be a little bit more difficult. So I just decided to do it myself. The good news is we had an enormous amount of success last year with that strategy. However, it is not a sustainable framework. It just isn't. If I had my druthers what I would like to see would be a situation in which I have a very engaging and aggressive change agent leading that space.

This is an ongoing challenge for the smaller HBCUs—those with endowments below $20 million—as the lack of resources required to assemble a high-performing development operation, is just not available (Gasman & Anderson-Thompkins, 2003). However, as mentioned earlier, fully functional development operations are typically not turn-key units, but rather projects that start with a vision and a strong commitment from the administrative team. While this brick-by-brick approach will take time, history tells us that all journeys begin with the first step.

VISIBILITY

Although there are risks involved, one of the best ways to draw the attention of the media, funders, and individuals with influence and wealth is by speaking out publicly on important issues. Throughout history there have been HBCU presidents who were highly vocal. These leaders include individuals such as Benjamin E. Mays of Morehouse College. Mays was born to former slaves in 1894. Inspired by some of the Black community's great intellectuals and orators, including Frederick Douglas, Booker T. Washington, and Paul Laurence Dunbar, Mays became a Baptist minister and eventually earned a Ph.D. from the University of Chicago (Mays, 2003). The stalwart "spiritual mentor" of Martin Luther King Jr. was vocal in both the Atlanta community and across the nation. He wrote articles and op-eds, gave speeches in national venues, and was quite controversial in his approach (Mays, 2003; Carter, 1998).

Likewise, Johnnetta B. Cole, the president of both Spelman College and Bennett College for Women, was also an outspoken HBCU leader. Cole is an anthropologist who earned her Ph.D. at Northwestern University. She did her undergraduate work at Fisk University and Oberlin College—two institutions known for instilling a sense of responsibility and justice in their students. These two institutions, along with the influence of her parents, shaped her brave and outspoken commitment to advancing the lives of African Americans and issues of social justice (Cole, 1994). Like Mays, she wrote op-eds for national venues and authored a book on sexism among African

Americans, entitled *Gender Talk* (2003), while president and in the midst of successful fundraising campaigns. She took a chance as some funders might have recoiled after reading her perspectives, which pushed back at gender relations among Blacks in America. Cole's forthright, confident nature and her ability to capture national attention assisted with Spelman's fundraising success (Barrett, 2006; Gasman, 2001).

Johnnetta Cole and Benjamin Mays are considered by most in the HBCU community, as well as by researchers, as premier HBCU presidents. Some have even labeled them aberrations, showing immense courage and strength often in the midst of an environment that did not support the education of Blacks. Although speaking out, in our opinion, should be in the lexicon of skills held by all college and university presidents, it is not always the case. Regardless, within the HBCU context there are myriad examples of presidents who demonstrate bravery and speak out, gaining visibility for their institutions.

One may look at the examples of Mays and Cole and think, 'Okay, you have a point, but these presidents are at the premier HBCUs—the ones that everyone knows about, that's not possible at other HBCUs.' Not true. There are presidents from lesser known HBCUs, even those that have struggled, who have taken a chance and spoken out. Walter Kimbrough, the president of Philander Smith College in Little Rock, Arkansas, regularly writes op-eds and has blogged about HBCUs for *The New York Times*. Kimbrough is the 12th president of Philander Smith College and is one of the youngest presidents in the country. He pursued his undergraduate degree at the University of Georgia and a Ph.D. at Georgia State University. Before becoming president of Philander Smith College, Kimbrough served as the vice president of student affairs. Upon becoming president, Kimbrough was tagged the "Hip Hop" president by news outlets. Kimbrough also authored a best-selling and somewhat controversial book entitled *Black Greek 101: The Culture, Customs and*

Challenges of Black Fraternities and Sororities (2003). Of note, Kimbrough has not stayed clear of controversy in his op-eds or his comments to the press. He has taken on *US News and World Report's* ranking of college and universities, especially HBCUs. For example, in 2007, Kimbrough spoke out in a *Diverse: Issues in Higher Education* article about the rankings, stating "If there are people looking at the rankings as a measurement of the quality of an institution, they think [HBCUs] do not have any type of qualities. The rankings do not tell you who the best schools are, just the most privileged" (Kimbrough in Kamara, 2007b, n.p.). In addition to speaking out in *Diverse*, Kimbrough participated in a letter writing campaign sponsored by Education Conservancy to convince HBCU presidents to boycott the *USNEWS* rankings. At the time that Kimbrough pushed for the boycott, he was a new HBCU president and did not have the political clout among HBCU leaders to gain widespread approval. Speaking out brought greater visibility to his campus.

In an op-ed in *Inside Higher Education*, Kimbrough has questioned whether giving to rich, Ivy League institutions that perpetuate privilege is really philanthropy (2007a, n.p.). Specifically, Kimbrough stated:

> On April 11, the president of Columbia University announced that it had received a $400 million pledge from alumnus John W. Kluge, who in 2006 was 52nd on the *Forbes* list of the wealthiest people, earning his fortune through the buying and selling of television and radio stations. This gift, payable upon the 92-year-old's death, will be the fourth largest ever given to a single institution of higher education. With such a massive transfer of wealth, the accolades poured in, justifying such a gift to an Ivy League university. Columbia's president, Lee Bollinger, said: "The essence of America's greatness lies, in no small measure, in our collective commitment to giving all people the opportunity to improve their lives ... [Kluge] has chosen to direct his amazing generosity to ensuring that young people will have the chance to benefit from

a Columbia education regardless of their wealth or family income." Mayor Michael Bloomberg indicated that investing in education produces returns that can't be matched. Rep. Charles Rangel said the gift would ensure greater numbers of students can afford a first-class education. Oh please!

Kimbrough took a hard swing at the nation's wealthy philanthropists that give to elite institutions He elaborated on the above:

> I am becoming less and less tolerant of people who pass wealth on to the privileged and masquerade it as philanthropy. Philanthropy is the voluntary act of donating money, goods or services to a charitable cause, intended to promote good or improve human well-being. When a billionaire gives money that will benefit people who are more than likely already well off or who already have access to huge sums of money, attending the ninth richest university by endowment, this is not philanthropy. This simply extends the gross inequities that exist in our country—inequities that one day will come home to roost (n.p.).

In speaking out so vehemently, Kimbrough took a calculated risk—one that could have resulted in foundations and philanthropist shunning him and his institution or could have brought him respect from many different constituents including funders. His risk paid off.

Kimbrough is also quite forthright when answering the media's inquiries about his leadership and HBCUs overall. He does not try to hide from the media and is upfront about Philander Smith College's performance indicators, sharing data, even when the data need improvement. In turn the media respects him and have given him and his institution a good amount of positive press (Redden, 2009; Masterson, 2010).

Kimbrough's visibility in the media has caught the attention of funders. They see a president who is brave, progressive, and not satisfied with the status quo. They also notice that he makes decisions based on evidence and have made significant grants to Philander Smith based on Kimbrough's actions and vision. One funder in particular, the Kresge Foundation, recently awarded Philanders Smith College a $1.2 million grant to support a center for social justice. When Kimbrough took on the leadership of the small college in Arkansas, he noticed that it did not have an institutional niche or anything truly unique about it. There were not majors or strengths for students and faculty to rally around. In an effort to increase enthusiasm on campus, elevate the reputation of Philander Smith College, and reach out to the local community, Kimbrough changed the school's motto to "Think Justice." He focused the campus energy on social justice and wove the notion throughout the curriculum and co-curriculum. Most recently, a group of foundations known as the MSI Funders chose to visit Kimbrough's college in order to learn more about HBCUs and their leadership. In their opinion, Kimbrough exemplifies the kind of bravery and leadership skills needed to be president of an HBCU in the 21st Century.

Charlie Nelms, the chancellor of North Carolina Central University, has also demonstrated bravery. In 2010, he held a public discussion about the future of HBCUs, encouraging an open and honest conversation about the challenges that HBCUs face. He brought together prominent researchers, including experts on retention, leadership, and fundraising, to push HBCUs forward. Nelms held this conversation publicly in front of funders and the media and as a result of his willingness to discuss tough issues and identify possible results, he has secured additional funding as well as some positive press (Kelderman, 2010). Eric Kelderman of the *Chronicle of Higher Education* highlighted the challenges that HBCUs face, but also applauded the HBCU leaders for their frank discussion. Charlie Nelms was lauded for his courage to have the discussion as well as his institution's efforts to create a "university college" to cater to the needs of first year students. Nelms's boldness and openness were the highlight of the *Chronicle* article with Eric Kelderman quoting him at the conclusion of the piece: "If we're [HBCUs] going to be around as a group of institutions 25 years from now, we have to change our narrative and our approach and be strategic."

Another president who has been using his role to make positive change is Michael Sorrell, the president of Paul Quinn College. Sorrell holds a J.D. from Duke and up until recently, he was a corporate attorney. He decided to take on the leadership role at Paul Quinn despite being advised not to by all of his friends and mentors. In order to save this struggling college, Sorrell has resorted to some innovative and slightly unorthodox strategies. For example, he turned an unused football field into an organic farm. He also secured a donation to demolish 13 abandoned buildings on the Paul Quinn campus. Sorrell could have done this work in isolation. However, he chose not to and instead made the media aware of his efforts, writing op-eds for various Dallas, Texas papers (Sorrel, 2010). By doing this, Sorrell has been able to drum up interest from those in Dallas who had given up on the institution. He has been transparent about the problems on his campus and contextualizes them by describing the state and national climate for higher education in his discussions of Paul Quinn.

Most recently, Sorrell wrote an op-ed for the *Dallas News* that focused on his institution's rocky past and where he is taking it in the future. Specifically, he proclaimed:

> No longer are we prisoners to negative experiences and missteps that occurred 10 to 15 years ago. We have closed that chapter of our history. Today, we celebrate a new truth, a new perception and a new reality. The work being done by the Paul Quinn family is critically important not only to Dallas, but also to under-resourced communities across the country. We are developing a model for others to embrace and replicate. Each member of the Paul Quinn family acknowledges that we

still have work to do to become one of America's great small colleges. Somewhere in the Paul Quinn experience is the following advice and an offer for those who cling desperately and rigidly to outdated perceptions and allow those perceptions to define their realities: Stop living in the past. If you will start seeing us for who we are today, we promise to do the same for you.

Rather than let the locals in Dallas, who could be potential donors, harbor feelings about the college based on past information, Sorrell took responsibility for the institution's missteps and pushed forward a new agenda for the college and its students. He made the education of low-income, first generation students a priority rather than his own ego. This approach has paid off in terms of support from citizens of Dallas, Texas funders, and alumni.

Each of these presidents spoke out in support of HBCUs in order to bolster the education of African Americans. In doing so, the presidents also elevated the reputations of their institutions.

Another method of speaking out on issues and making one's institution more visible is through policy papers that are disseminated to policymakers, funders, the media, and those in higher education. Mary Sias, president of Kentucky State University, George Wright, president of Prairie View A&M University, and Ron Mason, president of the Southern University of Louisiana System recently co-authored a policy paper on HBCUs and graduation rates. The paper challenged conventional methods for calculating graduation rates as these methods privilege colleges and universities that accept highly prepared, affluent students. When controlling for income and academic preparation, the presidents argued that HBCUs graduation rates are comparable and often surpass those of many similar historically White institutions. The policy paper received considerable media attention. And, the sponsoring organization, the Thurgood Marshall College Fund shared it with those at the Department of Education and the White House Initiative on HBCUs in an attempt to change the way the federal government assesses college attainment levels (Ashley et al., 1999). When HBCU presidents author policy papers on important issues related to HBCUs, it shows a commitment to improving and a willingness to confront difficult questions. They also gain respect.

Perhaps the most vocal president of an HBCU is Julianne Malveaux. Prior to becoming president of Bennett College for Women, Malveaux was a journalist, writing regular columns for *USA TODAY*, *Ms. Magazine*, and *Essence*. Coming to the presidency, she was chock full of writing experience and was not afraid to speak out—she had been doing it for decades and in a very provocative and public way. Malveaux also has a Ph.D. from MIT in economics and this gives her considerable credibility with the media as she rarely makes an argument without a treasure trove of statistics to back up her assertions.

Unlike most of the HBCU presidents mentioned in this chapter, Malveaux speaks out publically on many issues that are not directly related to HBCUs or higher education, including health care, gender and racial inequity, and unemployment. She doesn't bite her tongue often. When Malveaux was appointment president of Bennett College some in the HBCU community were surprised. As mentioned, she had been an opinionated journalist. Although the institution's previous president, Johnnetta B. Cole, was also outspoken, she was much more of a traditional academic in her approach. Malveaux is an in-your-face president and is not afraid to speak her mind. According to a story in *Diverse: Issues in Higher Education*, "some academics familiar with her often-polarizing punditry wonder if her hard-charging style will mesh well with the demands put upon a college president" (Pluvoise, 2007). When she first arrived at Bennett, the board tried to limit her public persona and her op-ed writing. That did not last long and within a year, Malveaux was back writing provocative op-eds.

In 2009, for example, she wrote an op-ed in the *Chicago Defender* in which she poked and prodded at Republicans and their dislike of Barack Obama's health care plan. Although she nicely laid out the reasons why some Americans oppose health care reform, Malveaux also took several pot shots at Republicans—both the leaders and the masses. Malveaux asks important social-justice-oriented questions, such as "We know there are 50 million uninsured adults and children. What kind of productivity drain exists because people don't have the health insurance they need?" Perhaps her most controversial claim was that the real reason for Republicans' dislike of health care reform is that they dislike Barack Obama. Many college and university presidents stay clear of aligning themselves publically with political parties, but Malveaux makes her stance clear. Although to be fair, she has been very critical of Obama's actions as president as well. College presidents need to choose whether or not they want to venture into political territory to gain visibility.

In another op-ed, written for the *Seattle Medium*, Malveaux took on the issue of gender inequity. Speaking as the president of Bennett College, Malveaux argued that the African American community as well as the nation as a whole must come together and support the success and aspirations of women. In her words:

> We must claim this month [women's history month], not simply as a statement of history, but also as an opportunity to remind the nation and the world that gender equity is a human imperative. In other words, we don't just want pay equity for women, but we want pay equity for families and for a nation. When women aren't well paid, families aren't well cared for. When women are kicked to the curb economically, children suffer and we experience generational reverberations. Fair treatment of women is an investment in the growth, development, and success of our nation (Malveaux, 2011).

Because she is president of a women's college, Malveaux's voice on issues related to gender equity appear to be directly linked to her position and expertise.

RESPONDING TO CONTROVERSY AND INCREASING VISIBILITY

On September 28, 2010, Jason L. Riley, an op-ed writer for the *Wall Street Journal*, penned an article entitled "Black Colleges Need a New Mission." In the article, Riley relied on the dated perspective of scholars writing in the 1960s and 70s and those that compare HBCUs to Ivy League institutions (Sowell, 1972; Jencks & Riesman, 1967). In making this comparison, Riley failed to realize that there are few public or private institutions in the United States that stand up to those comparisons in terms of endowment size and other factors. Riley's judgments are patently unfair and undermine any serious discussions of the true value of HBCUs. A fair assessment of the work of HBCUs places them side by side with historically White institutions (HWIs) with similar student populations. Specifically, HBCUs should be compared to institutions in Southern states with like percentages of Pell Grant eligible students and like SAT scores. Such an evaluation would show that in many cases HBCUs are doing a better job of educating African American students. Moreover, they have done so with far fewer resources than their HWI counterparts (Gasman, 2010b). One of the stinging problems with Riley's op-ed is its placement in the *Wall Street Journal*, a well-known paper with a healthy circulation. Within hours of being published, the op-ed went viral, making its way around HBCU and higher education circles. In looking at the on-line commentary responding to the article, it was evident that Riley touched a nerve. Riley, an African American editorial board member at the *Wall Street Journal*, gave the anti-HBCU crowd plenty of ammunition to use against these historic institutions and lit a fire under HBCU leaders across the country.

One of the first HBCU presidents to respond to Riley was William R. Harvey, the president of Hampton University in Virginia. Harvey received his undergraduate degree at Talladega College and his doctoral degree at Harvard University. Along with his leadership of Hampton, Harvey is the chair of the board of directors of the White House Initiative on Historically Black Colleges and Universities. He has been a hugely successful president, having served in this role since 1978. He has not only ensured the institution's financial security, but has pushed for more research and academic excellence across the faculty and student body.

In Harvey's (2010) op-ed, he noted the inconsistencies and inaccuracies in Riley's arguments. Harvey pointed toward the economic impact of HBCUs on the nation as a whole and also highlighted their role in providing jobs. For example, HBCUs have a national economic impact of $10 billion annually and provide 180,000 jobs. Harvey also pushed back hard at Riley's assertion that HBCUs should bring in for profit institutions such as the University of Phoenix to manage them. Specifically, he stated "Does he really want HBCUs to model themselves after an institution whose latest graduation rates as reported by the Integrated Postsecondary Education Data System (IPEDS), was 1 percent at 4 years, 4 percent at 6 years, and 6 percent at 8 years?" (n.p.). Because of Harvey's stature within the HBCU world and among the nation's political leaders and policymakers, his voice was a vital part of the rebuttal to Riley.

Another voice of defense for HBCUs was David Wilson, the newly-minted president of Morgan State University in Maryland. Wilson is the 12th president of Morgan State and prior to holding the position he served as the chancellor of the University of Wisconsin Colleges and University of Wisconsin-Extension. He attended Tuskegee University for his undergraduate degree and Harvard for his doctoral degree. Although Wilson was only in the Morgan presidency for a few months, he spoke out vehemently against Riley's perspective. The *Washington Afro* published his opinion. Wilson pointed to the inaccuracies in Riley's arguments much like Harvey did, but he also drew on his experience at historically White institutions. According to Wilson, "I have attended and worked at a number of tradition- ally White institutions and can testify to the fact that little stands between them and HBCUs, save that which a large endowment will buy." He urged Riley to "compare HBCUs with other schools of their size and nature, and not just to the most elite of col- leges and universities in the country." In addition, he noted "If he is going to compare HBCUs to the Harvards and MITS of the world, then he also must compare those schools with the smaller, less well-endowed, traditionally White institutions" (n.p.).

In addition to this op-ed article, David Wilson has been vocal at HBCU-focused conferences. In April 2011, for exam- ple, he served on a panel at the National Press Club that fea- tured Richard Vedder, a critic of HBCUs, and members of the Black and HBCU communities. The panel was sponsored by the National Association for Equal Opportunity (NAFEO) and was meant to be a direct response to the HBCU critics who have surfaced over the past year. At the event, Wilson was quite vocal, giving a response that he claimed was not a response to Vedder, but merely an overview of the strength of HBCUs. He told the audience that there is no reason to defend HBCUs. In his talk, Wilson discussed the many strengths of Morgan State University. For example, Morgan is ranked second in Maryland in the percentage of its students who graduate and go on to graduate school—a percentage that is higher than the state's flagship institution, University of Maryland. Speaking out early in his presidency and so vehemently has raised Wilson's profile nationwide.

The last president to write an op-ed in response to Jason Riley (although she did not name him) was Beverly Daniel Tatum. Tatum is the president of Spelman College in Atlanta. She holds a bachelor's degree from Wesleyan University and a Ph.D. from the University of Michigan. Prior to taking the lead at Spelman, Tatum served as the dean and acting president of Mount Holyoke College. Tatum is probably best known for her book *Why Are All the Black Kids Sitting Together in the Cafeteria? And Other Conversations About Race* (1997). She is a consistent and vocal supporter of HBCUs and also a national commentator on racial issues and this greatly benefits Spelman.

Tatum opened her op-ed with examples of the many accolades that her students receive—Luce Fellowships to study child prostitution in Northern Thailand, Fulbright Scholarships to explore women and democracy in India, and the grand prize in the AT&T Big Mobile on Campus Challenge. She used these examples to point to the disconnect between Jason Riley's assessment of HBCUs as inferior and her own daily experiences leading Spelman. Tatum also took issue with Riley's commentary on HBCU SAT scores. Riley claimed that HBCU student SAT scores were an indication of the poor quality of the students and for that matter, HBCUs overall. In her words,

> It has been suggested by some commentators that the fact that average SAT scores are lower at Spelman than at equally selective institutions is an indicator of lower academic quality. I would suggest perhaps it is an indicator of lower average family income. SAT scores are more highly correlated with family income than almost any other variable—the higher the income, the higher the score is likely to be. According to a 2007 article in *Postsecondary Education Opportunity*, Spelman College is now educating more Pell Grant eligible students than any other selective liberal arts college in the nation, except Berea College. Of approximately 2,200 students at Spelman that year, 885 of them were Pell Grant recipients, 40 percent of our total population. Ivy League institutions with thousands more undergraduates are educating far fewer Pell Grant recipients. In 2008, Harvard had 543 among an undergraduate population of 6,700, Yale had 469 among 5,350, Princeton

only 264 among 4,719. Despite a much smaller endowment than these giants, it is Spelman College that is doing the important work of providing social mobility to talented students like these every year.

Unlike some of her presidential peers, Tatum is armed with an arsenal of data that she can use to defend the reputation of HBCUs and raise their visibility. Of course, Tatum was upfront about the fact that Spelman College is the most highly ranked HBCU and has the strongest endowment. She said, "I know that not every HBCU shares the same profile of Spelman College, nor does every majority institution look like Harvard. Yet it is important to understand each institution in its own context— its history, the region it serves, and the service it still provides to a nation in need of every source of talent" (2010, n.p.).

Although these responses are admirable, what HBCU presidents need to do is to take a proactive approach to promoting the reputations of their institutions instead of reacting to criticism. In addition, like Beverly Tatum, HBCU presidents need to stay abreast of the current empirical literature that supports the contributions that HBCU make in order to promote the success of HBCUs with more than mere anecdotal stories. Being visible as a president leads to increased exposure among funders.

Black college presidents operate in a volatile environment in which their institutions are held suspect and questioned on a regular basis. As they are tuition-driven and highly dependent on consistent enrollment, they cannot take chances in terms of funding. Losing a funder as a result of speaking out on controversial issues is not an option for many HBCU presidents. Despite the potential risks involved, our research shows that those HBCU presidents who are more vocal and speak out publically are often the most successful. They attract the attention of policymakers and funders. They are seen as brave and command respect. In addition, funders see them as innovative and having a willingness to confront challenges. Lastly, presidents who speak out against injustice are seen as having a sense of integrity that is worth supporting.

THE PRESIDENT AND BOARDS OF TRUSTEES

According to a 2002 report by Ayers & Associates, HBCUs lack consistent trustee involvement in the monetary support of their institutions as well as assistance with fundraising. Unfortunately, this lack of involvement does not bode well for HBCUs as institutions that are most successful in terms of fundraising tend to be those with high levels of trustee involvement (Schultz, 2005; Gasman & Anderson-Thompkins, 2003).

One of the challenges for a new president and his or her advancement team is managing a board of trustees that was selected by the previous president. Within the HBCU context, if private, the board can consist of too many clergy members, who often lack access to funds as well as others who do not have a high giving capacity. If a public HBCU, the board is often appointed, at least in part, by the governor and these political appointees do not necessarily have access to resources. In order to maximize giving potential HBCU boards of trustees need to consist of individuals with access to funds or with connections to those with wealth. When a board is not made up of these types of people, the institution is handicapped in its fundraising efforts. The optimal board is made up of a diverse group of individuals, including people of various racial and ethnic backgrounds and genders. These individuals should have far reaching contacts and preferably, access to wealth.

Philander Smith College's board of trustees exemplifies diversity in its make-up. The institution has a 20-person board and half of those individuals have to be United Methodist given the institution's history. Half of the board is made up of alumni. The current board chair is a White male banker from the Little Rock area who is tightly connected to local wealth and influential people in the area.

Board members need to understand their role and it is the job of the president to educate them. Too often board members want to be involved in an institution but are not willing to make a commitment to moving the institution forward. The presidents of HBCUs, as well as the Board of Trustees chair, need to communicate the purpose of board membership to all individuals on the board. Clear expectations need to be established and communicated from the beginning of board service. According to Schultz (2005), "Trustees need to understand the tough and critical factors that hinder the viability of HBCUs. They need to understand their critical roles in assuring the financial viability with and beyond fundraising" (p. 17). The most successful presidents in terms of securing support from their trustees are those who take the time to educate them about the role of a trustee. Sometimes this education can take considerable time and talent.

According to one HBCU president, "One of the things that has happened in my view at my school is that we had people on our board who liked the institution and cared for it on an emotional level but they didn't invest in it." In other cases, board members think that it is their role to tell the president what to do on a daily basis rather than take an active role in fundraising. Charlie Nelms, the chancellor of North Carolina Central University sees the role of board members as being threefold:

> First, they should be advocates for the institution within the legislative process in North Carolina. Secondly, they should be able to identify persons within their network or through their relationships who we can then work on cultivating and eventually soliciting donors. And third, they should have a willingness to participate in actual solicitations.

Although Nelms does not have the exact board in place that he desires yet, he is appointing individuals that are moving him closer to his goal.

When Walter Kimbrough arrived at Philander Smith College, only 30 percent of the board of trustees gave to the institution on a yearly basis. After considerable education and a change in expectations, 100 percent of the board gives. In Kimbrough's words,

> We've been at 100 percent for the last three years now and we have everyone giving. Now the next goal for us is to get them to give at a much greater level—for them to really start to not just give a donation—but to invest in the college. We have to change their mentality about being on the board.

Kimbrough wants his board to move from being satisfied with merely giving a gift to the institution ($100–$500 level) to investing in the college at the $1000 plus level. In order to increase the board's capacity, Kimbrough and his advancement staff have sought out individuals who have greater capacity to give. He has also sought out African Americans with their own family foundations and has found this to be a lucrative strategy (Gasman, 2010a). According to Kimbrough, "it is important to have alumni on the board but you can't rely on alumni who do not have a willingness or capacity to give."

Recently, Philander Smith College put a new board policy in place that states that all board members will be donors. The policy also recommends that board members give at the 1877 level, which is the lowest level of a major gift at the institution (and also the date of the college's founding). Kimbrough and his vice president Shannon Fleming recently pushed their board to give at a higher rate. They were able to get four board members to agree to a $2000 gift over four years and to ask other board members to do the same at a board meeting. Fleming describes this effort as "the biggest effort to strong arm the board we've attempted. We were trying to shift the mindset of the board." When we interviewed him for this book, Fleming was in the early planning stages of a campaign. Of note, he was planning on asking his board to be responsible for 10 percent of the quiet phase of the fundraising campaign—by giving the monies themselves or securing the funds from others. According to Fleming, "this is going to be another pivotal moment for our board in terms of their commitment."

As noted, presidents of public institutions are in a particularly precarious position when it comes to boards as these entities are often appointed by the governor of the state. The governor may or may not be supportive of HBCUs and in fact might be hostile. For example, most recently, the governors of both Mississippi and Louisiana spoke out against public HBCUs, calling for their consolidation or worse yet, elimination. Oftentimes the boards of public HBCUs are filled with appointees with little knowledge about or interest in HBCUs. One president of a public Black college whom we interviewed stated, "I have to be careful with my board because most of the people were not selected by me. They were appointed by the governor and the prior president." This president expressed frustration that his board was not a "giving board." Prior to his arrival at the university, the board was not required to give, do any fundraising, or secure prospects. They served as an oversight entity rather than a supportive board. In cases like this, the president often needs to wait out the board members' terms and strategically identify different board members for the future.

One vice president of Advancement who works at a public HBCU worked to make his non-giving board a giving board through constant badgering. He called board members and told them that giving was non-negotiable. His tactic included telling board members that they were the only ones that had not given. Although this is not a strategy that we would recommend, 'shaming' has been used by many colleges and universities to cajole alumni, board members, and even students into giving. In the case of board members, heavy persuasion is more acceptable given the role that these individuals take on. However, high pressure tactics with alumni can backfire and the use of these strategies with students has been heavily criticized (Strom, 2010).

Although Robert Franklin at Morehouse College does not use "shaming," he is willing to have tough conversations with board members who are not pulling their weight in terms of fundraising. In terms of board giving, Morehouse has three tiers. There are the corporate individuals from whom Franklin is very clear that he expects a seven-figure gift. In Morehouse's latest campaign he expected them to give in the $3 to $5 million range. The second tier includes nonprofit leadership. This tier is made up of former college presidents, clergy, and other leaders. According to Franklin, "we look at this group broadly. We are interested in their reach. We ask them for $10,000 annually but we also ask them to consider us in the church budgets if they are clergy." The third tier includes retired individuals who are on the board due to their wisdom and the power of their endorsement. Although Franklin has not "kicked anyone off the board" for not giving or assisting with fundraising, he has had very serious conversations with board members about their lack of productivity when it comes to fundraising. As a result, a few board members have decided not to serve any longer.

At the opposite end of the spectrum from Morehouse College is Paul Quinn College. The Dallas-based college's president Michael Sorrell has monetary expectations of his board but because his institution is struggling, he has to be very creative in using his board's resources. According to Sorrell,

> We expect board members to give $5000 a year but that donation can be in non-monetary gifts. Recent non-monetary gifts included American Airlines providing complimentary tickets for the staff and a law firm that is representing Paul Quinn in its fight for accreditation. It's an evolutionary process for us. Our board is really becoming

a much better board in terms of fundraising. In fairness, we're doing a much better job of making specific asks.

Sorrell noted that he is being very clear about his needs in terms of resources, introductions, and relationship building. He is also educating his board in terms of speaking up and offering more assistance.

Overall, presidents need to ensure that their boards of trustees are diverse in make-up and diverse in skills and talents. They also need to create meaningful ways for board members to be involved beyond mere meetings, drawing on the expertise of the individual members. For example, board members can help with donor identification and stewardship. Presidents also need to communicate the institution's case to the board and make sure that it can then communicate the institution's mission and case to others, including viable fundraising prospects. Opening lines of communication and setting high expectations leads to a more effective board of trustees and a stronger fundraising strategy.

HIRING AND EMPOWERING THE BEST PEOPLE

Of utmost importance to the effectiveness of a fundraising program and the president's role in the program is the hiring of highly talented people. The president needs to hire individuals with far reaching connections, charisma, and innovative ideas and then let them do their jobs. Of course oversight is essential, but trusting those in advancement to lead the way to success is vital to empowering these individuals to do their best work. A president that exemplifies this attitude and approach is Walter Kimbrough at Philander Smith College. He hired Shannon Fleming, a White male who had served as the associate vice president at Central Arkansas University. Although Central Arkansas is quite different than Philander Smith, namely it is larger and is not an HBCU, Fleming possesses a skill set that is essential in the region. When it comes to building the Advancement Department, according to Kimbrough, "Fleming took the lead in terms of the kind of people we needed for the team." Kimbrough wanted his vice president to take ownership of the department and to hire people who complemented the needs of the institution.

Charlie Nelms at North Carolina Central also believes in hiring the best person for the job regardless of their racial and ethnic background or institution history. In his words,

> There's a tendency sometimes at HBCUs, at my HBCU, I won't generalize about all, there's a reluctance, it seems to me, to hire people who are not HBCU graduates on the one hand and persons who may not necessarily have worked at HBCUs on the other. My attitude is that I want the best talent I can find. That's what I want. I also want people who have a sensitivity to the mission of my HBCU. So it's talent and sensitivity that we're looking for and that is not always embraced by some of my colleagues.

Once Nelms gets these talented individuals in place, he empowers them to do their job and respects their expertise in the field. An example of Nelms's willingness to hire the best person for the job comes in a recent hire he made. According to Nelms,

> I think minorities can relate to people of all ethnicities and races. I think it helps to have a more diverse staff in institutional advancement because there are some people who appear to be more receptive to interacting with certain people than others. And so what I did was retain the services of a Caucasian man, who had previously been the public affairs director for Verizon as well as the president of the local chamber of commerce. I brought him on board sensing that we did not have the kind of contacts that we needed with the majority community in this region of the state. And so it was through him that we were able

to set up conversations with [wealthy majority people and these relationships resulted in tangible gifts]."

James Anderson, the chancellor of Fayetteville State University, empowers his advancement staff by giving his "absolute support." According to Anderson,

> Whenever they need me, whenever they call on me, I am there. I am willing to make a trip anywhere; I am willing to talk with anyone that they need me to talk to. I never leave that to a secondary person if it's necessary for me to do it.

Unfortunately not all presidents come into the position with ample fundraising experience and as a result, some shy away from the fundraising aspect of their job. This makes for a frustrating experience for the advancement staff because they need a highly engaged president.

WHAT IF THE PRESIDENT ISN'T ENGAGED?

Presidents are extremely busy people, being pulled in multiple directions by faculty, students, donors, and boards of trustees. They often focus on what is immediately in front of them. It is important to keep the financial strength, in terms of fundraising possibilities, in front of the president at all times. The unengaged president is more likely to be found at a public HBCU because these institutions, much like their historically White counterparts, have only been raising substantial funds for the past couple decades (Tindall, 2007). At some public HBCUs, the development office merely act as a repository for funds that came to the institution rather than a department that initiates solicitations and strategies for financial strength (Tindall, 2007).

Some HBCU presidents do not properly weigh institutional priorities to maximize their ability to raise funds. For example, we know of instances at which presidents have chosen not to attend prominent national meetings at which both public and private funders were in attendance; instead choosing a more local gathering involving sports or just not attending due to lack of interest. In difficult economic times as well as those that are prosperous, HBCUs cannot afford to bypass opportunities to be in a room with funders. Participating in meetings populated with funders puts the president at the table, engaging in conversations with those who can support the institution. In an environment in which HBCUs are constantly questioned as to their continued existence, telling one's institutional story to those who can sustain it is vital.

If a president is not engaged, it is still possible to secure his or her attention. For example, an advancement officer can invite the president and other top level administrators to development trainings to sharpen the president's skills in the fundraising area. Another strategy is to engage the president with the help of a prominent alumnus. Hearing about the importance of engagement from an alumnus can be convincing. It is important to prepare the alumnus, noting the need for increased engagement on the part of the president. The advancement staff members also need to make sure presidents understand their integral role in fundraising, empowering them to embrace this aspect of their job. We talked with one development officer who spent considerable time, almost two years, convincing his president that fundraising was part of her job. The president saw her role as being more internal and was highly resistant to asking donors for money and traveling on a regular basis. The development officer eventually called on a prominent donor, who worked with the president to put her at ease in terms of fundraising.

COUNTERPRODUCTIVE PRESIDENTS

In some instances, the president, although having made the decision to work hand in hand with the development office and having agreed to meet regularly to exchange ideas, will side-step the fundraising professionals and choose to enter the solicitation alone and unprepared. This often leads to an over-ask and worst still, an under-ask based on future promises. For example, we learned of one situation in which a president was scheduled to visit a city where a prominent alumnus and consistent donor resided. Before leaving campus, the president instructed his administrative assistant to set up a meeting with the alumnus. During the meeting, the graduate mentioned having included a six-figure gift to the university in his estate plan. Recognizing the alumnus was in the later stages of life, the president, assumed the gift would come sooner than later. In addition to this assumption, the president failed to gain general counsel approval on legal documents and offered a naming opportunity to the donor. Months later, upon receiving the completed estate documents, a university staff attorney recognized a clause that would delay the university's receipt of the gift until after all surviving family members of the donor's family had passed away, including the donor's mother, wife, and three children, ranging in age from 35 to 50. As a result, the agreement was made, the naming ceremony completed, and the donor's name was prominently placed on the building even though, six years later, he was still very much alive.

If presidents are going to be most useful, they must spend considerable time working to understand the institution's short- and long-term fundraising goals, and how they can support the overall strategic plan. Ongoing collaborations with the development office to gain a full orientation on potential donors—previous giving history, interest, and capacity levels—can prevent the premature under-selling of the institution's limited assets.

Another counterproductive measure on the part of many presidents is allowing personal and emotional feelings about donors to cloud the big picture of securing funding for the institution. Oftentimes, this occurs when the president is not a graduate of the institution of which he or she presides and therefore does not share the same sentiments as many alumni. Many alumni have an "I know what's best for the University" type of mentality that becomes exponentially amplified once they become donors. The research shows that this passion is consistent among HBCU and Predominately White Institution (PWI) graduates and with that, presidents need to understand this type of zeal (which can manifest as critique) does exist and not view it as an indictment on their managerial ability. In most cases, it is a lack of understanding on the part of the donor as to the overall goal of the school. So often, these differences can be cleared up and agreed to with further discussions and concessions. Being flexible and allowing for wiggle room is paramount within financial negotiations and institutional leaders must embrace this and not internalize decisions based on personality differences.

The president plays the most important role in fundraising at HBCUs in several ways. First, he or she is the best advertisement for the institution—a "living logo" as stated earlier. Second, he or she has the ability to attract prominent individuals to the board who can contribute funds and secure funds from others. Third, the president can empower advancement staff in their roles, giving them more influence campus-wide. And lastly, presidents can bring all campus constituents into the fundraising process, including faculty, student affairs staff, students, and alumni.

Practical Recommendations

- Convince the president of his or her centrality to the fundraising process and the transformational nature of that role.
- Attract the attention of non-alumni donors by having the institution's president speak out on national issues in meaningful and thoughtful ways.

- Maximize the potential of the board and rebuild it if it lacks potential. Push board members to fulfill their obligation to the institution.
- Hire the most talented fundraisers, invest in their professional development, and let them do their job.
- Have regular meetings between the president and senior development staff to discuss donor strategy. Revisit this strategy regularly and build upon it.
- Think of every interaction and introduction to someone as a potential donation and follow up on each of these interactions.
- For the unengaged president, use high level donors to help with the engagement. Often high level donors can serve as a motivating source.

3

ACADEMIC DEANS, FACULTY, AND STUDENT SERVICES INVOLVEMENT

Oftentimes, academics see fundraising as "not their job" and also somewhat unsavory—they might compare it to the sales profession. Heaven forbid a faculty member would have to ask a donor for money. In this chapter, we focus on engaging the academic side of the HBCU in the fundraising process, showing deans and faculty how important a role they can play in the institution's sustainability and success. There are ample benefits to using an "all campus approach" to fundraising. For example, the partnership of fundraisers with faculty members brings together experts in a specific academic arena with experts in raising money for the institution. Although fundraisers are more adept at "making an ask," faculty members are the best equipped for discussing specific academic programs and initiatives—the partnership results in a mutually-beneficial situation. When the institutional advancement and academic sides of a college or university work together, they can combine efforts to prevent double solicitation of potential donors and coordinate ongoing communication. This communication may lead to more respect for the fundraising profession on the part of academic administrators and faculty members as well as a better understanding of academic programs and the needs of fundraisers.

There are significant advantages to involving faculty members in fundraising. They tend to have the closest and most positive relationships with students and, thus, are excellent ambassadors of the college or university. The positive feelings that students have for past faculty members lead to better feelings for the institution overall. Likewise, many faculty members maintain contact with students after they graduate, writing letters of recommendation and offering career advice. Oftentimes, faculty members have the most up to date information on students and they should be encouraged to share this with the advancement office. Of course, many faculty members are concerned with their own teaching or research so it is essential to make sure they are rewarded for their fundraising efforts. Fundraising is not their primary job and, as such, they should be given some kind of compensation for high level involvement, such as course releases, summer pay, and research or travel monies.

According to Hodson (2010), although "it is unrealistic to believe that all faculty and staff will become actively engaged in fundraising," their support of the institution's fundraising efforts is important to an HBCU's success (p. 42). Specifically, he notes, "Getting faculty involved in cultivation and solicitation of alumni and friends who admire their work or their commitment to the institution will enhance the likelihood that a request for financial support will be accepted" (p. 42).

On the ground, it can be difficult to involve faculty in fundraising. In the words of James Anderson of Fayettville State University, "Our academic side of the house does not have experience with fundraising. We need to conduct training sessions for deans and department chairs. These are the two groups of people who need to step up and do more fundraising." Arthur Affleck, the vice president of institutional advancement, uses the Council for the Advancement and Support of Education's (CASE) regional conferences to train his deans. He noted the benefits of "the formalized training process" at CASE. He has also had academics with experience in fundraising and grant writing come in and talk with deans and faculty. Hearing about the role of faculty in fundraising from an academic is often more palatable to faculty members. President Sorrell at Paul Quinn College suggests "taking baby steps" with faculty and feeling out their level of comfort and expertise in the fundraising area. Before faculty members are unleashed to raise money, they need to feel comfortable with the underlying concepts of fundraising.

To Anderson's point, most deans at HBCUs are not trained in fundraising, they are often uncomfortable asking for a gift from donors—even those donors who have longstanding relationships with their individual school, college, or program. According to Arthur Affleck,

> Because deans are new to fundraising, they often ask for gifts prematurely and on occasion in a clumsy way. Sometimes they are not on the same page with the development office and the strategy we envision for approaching a donor.

The worst that can happen is for a potential donor to be called by multiple entities at an institution. Affleck recalled this happening when he first came to Fayetteville State University. However, he worked hard to educate the deans about fundraising and bolster their self-confidence.

At some HBCUs, fundraising responsibilities are strongly encouraged by presidents at the individual school level, but are not obligatory. At other HBCUs, the lines are clearly drawn; fundraising is an institutional advancement activity and teaching and instruction are academic responsibilities—the two shall remain separate. The latter belief is not new to public HBCUs as they have had a long tradition of solely relying on federal and state revenue streams—funding that has been the life-line of these institutions throughout their histories.

At Prairie View A&M University (PVAMU), the fundraising staff uses an "all campus approach" in which all academic units are involved and are required to bring in a certain level of unrestricted dollars to the University annually. In 2008, the PVAMU administration began to recognize the potential benefits to be gained from faculty participation in fundraising. They implemented accountability measures for each academic unit, which required the creation of strategic fundraising plans with benchmarks to be met. These plans specified annual fundraising targets as well as the identification of alumni, corporations, and foundations that possess the capacity to make a major gift. To achieve their fundraising goals, the school deans or their designees were required to meet with the development office staff for guidance, attend development training sessions, and bring key faculty and staff into the fundraising process, thereby creating a sense of ownership. The efforts at PVAMU not only resulted in better institutional relationships across campus, but increased financial gains within each school.

For example, each academic unit at PVAMU had an individual goal and collectively the units exceeded the overall goal by 98 percent in 2010. Of note, all of the monies raised were unrestricted and could be used for such things as faculty and staff professional development, equipment purchases, and student travel. As a result of this success, President George Wright saw another area for which he wanted the academic units to raise funds— the Thurgood Marshall College Fund Leadership Conference. Each year, PVAMU takes 15–20 students to the leadership conference in New York City. These students are the best and brightest the university has to offer. However, in an attempt to ensure involvement from all academic areas, this year, each is required to raise funds for two of their own students to attend the conference. Wright considers New York City a great place to expose students to various cultural outlets related to their particular disciplines. For instance, music students can visit Carnegie Hall, business students can visit Wall Street, and architectural students can explore the city's many examples of modern design.

Like PVAMU, Morehouse College's advancement team has had some success working with faculty members. They worked with the science and math division at the institution to secure federal stimulus funds. They trained the faculty in grant writing, making sure that the college was smart about its applications and approach. They also found that the faculty members were eager to be more involved in raising institutional funds when they were prepared and had the appropriate resources. According to Morehouse President Franklin, he would like to have a larger fundraising staff so that they can spend more time working with faculty to bring in department-specific resources.

ENGAGING STUDENT SERVICES

What students experience in the various student services areas has a significant impact on their willingness to give back to their alma mater. According to Gasman and Anderson-Thompkins (2003), based on a myriad of interviews with HBCU alumni, the top reason why alumni do not give back to their alma maters is that they had a negative experience. If students are treated with respect while on campus, they tend to give back. If not, they often hold resentment toward the institution, which can lead to resistance toward giving.

Although customer service is basic, it has long been a problem at many HBCUs where resources are stretched thin and people are often doing too many jobs. According to Walter Kimbrough, the president of Philander Smith College and a former vice president of Student Affairs at Albany State University, Black colleges have a Bermuda Triangle in which students get lost. These students then become disgruntled alumni. The Bermuda Triangle consists mainly of the registrar, the business office, and financial aid. Students have bad experiences in these particular areas and harbor long-term negative feelings about these experiences and the individuals they encountered working in these areas.

A case in point involves students who would rather complete loan applications for aid rather than identify free scholarship assistance. According to some students "it's less of a hassle." When asked to explain their responses in more detail, these students said,

> while the counselors seem more than happy to hand you a loan application and tell you to complete and return it, when asked about scholarship opportunities, they instantly withdraw, assuming more of a gate-keeper mentality. It's like the scholarships belong to them—as if it is their money.

The research shows that at many HBCUs 85 percent or more of the student population is on some type of financial aid; and with the majority of students being first generation, low-income college attendees, those percentages are certainly understandable (Gasman & Tudico, 2008). Research also indicates that year after year, many HBCUs harbor un-awarded scholarships that could certainly be used to reduce the thousands of dollars of student debt that their students are saddled with following the completion and in some cases the non-completion of their undergrad degree. If the students' recap of their interaction with financial aid is to be believed, HBCUs need to do whatever they can to make sure that students are going to school with as much financial aid as possible, primarily scholarships. It is their obligation.

Morehouse College is an institution with a fairly strong rate of alumni giving—roughly 39 percent. However, President Franklin was not satisfied with the percentage and thought that customer service might be the key to increasing future alumni giving. He had heard complaints from students and alumni about the treatment they received from various units on campus. To strengthen the staff's customer services skills, he brought in a team from the Ritz Carlton Leadership Center for an all-day seminar. Franklin wanted to ensure that his staff appreciated their role in fundraising and its impact on future giving.

Jim Anderson of Fayetteville State sought to motivate all of his faculty and staff to understand their role in leaving a positive impression on future alumni. For the annual campus-wide opening session for the faculty and staff, he had them read *Pour Your Heart Into It: How Starbucks Built a Company One Cup at a Time*. His institution adopted the concept of "from ordinary to extraordinary" and not only sought to better the student services provided, but to remind students at every level that giving back to the institution is important.

Also at Fayetteville State University, they hired an outside firm to evaluate their customer service throughout the institution. According to Arthur Affleck, "Part of our conversation is about our brand promise and how we deliver on that promise. We are trying to make sure that everyone knows that they have one shot at making a first impression." Moreover, Affleck commented,

> One of the things that I have said to financial aid and admissions staff is "you are asked by students and parents for things that you can't do or are not able to do at that moment in time." I ask them to refrain from saying "no" on the first request. In fact, you should never say "no." Always say I'm not sure that we can do that but let me check. Let me see if there's a way. And honestly even if you know the answer is 'no' something may have happened that morning that you didn't know

about—for example, we may have gotten a big check in from somebody who says give it away right away.

One vice president of advancement relayed a story to us about the poor customer service in the registrar area at his institution. He noted,

> All of the staff members had their phones transferred somewhere else and there was no service for students. This lack of service made one newly-minted alumnus so angry that he told the president that he felt disrespected and mistreated when he visited or called the office. He vowed not to give to the institution.

According to those we interviewed, there is no reason to mistreat a student or alumnus and, in fact, doing so is counter intuitive in terms of future giving. In order to combat negative behavior, some schools use "secret shoppers" who visit various student services offices to see what kind of treatment they might receive. Good treatment is rewarded but bad treatment is reprimanded.

Those in the student services area at many HBCUs need to be held accountable for their behavior in order to bolster future alumni giving. However, accountability cannot come through mandates and top down directives. Student services employees need to be empowered to do their best work through an understanding of their role in educating and supporting HBCU students. Staff members, and faculty members, for that matter, need to understand that African American students have options and do not have an obligation to attend HBCUs. Basically, if students are not treated well, they will vote with their feet and this will result in a lack of jobs for those in student services. As it stands only 16 percent of African American students attend HBCUs as undergraduates (Gasman & Tudico, 2008).

Practical Recommendations

- Teach academic deans about their role in fundraising, providing them with professional development and guidance along the way.
- Convince faculty members of the role that they can play in engaging alumni by reminding them of the influence that they have on the lives of young people.
- Assess student services at your institution—business office, registrar's office, and financial aid—to ensure that students and alumni are well treated.
- Create a campus-wide initiative themed around empowering employees to modify their attitudes and behaviors toward students.
- Bring in outside sources to change or interrupt the status quo in the area of customer service.

4

ALUMNI GIVING AND ENGAGEMENT

Literature on alumni development suggests colleges and universities that attain significant alumni giving rates tend to have well developed and implemented strategies, with many focusing on developing current students into giving alumni.

Ayers & Associates, 2002

The marketplace of education has become increasingly competitive, forcing colleges and universities to rely more heavily on alumni to assist them in meeting their institutional goals (Baade & Sundberg, 1995; Weerts & Ronca, 2007; Willemain et al., 1994). According to Weerts & Ronca (2007), alumni have the potential to assist their alma maters in many ways, including volunteerism, charitable giving, and even political advocacy. On the surface, alumni represent the one constituency of higher education that would seemingly have the most allegiance and loyalty to colleges and universities (Gasman & Anderson-Thompkins, 2003; Wunnava & Lauze, 2000; Cohen, 2008). After all, their college experience preceded their professional career and, in many cases, helped to develop the specific skill-set graduates use in their daily vocations. And certainly, if you ask most alumni, they will swear their allegiance is forever to the Crimson and Gray or the Maroon and White as evidenced during homecoming or graduation. However, this same level of adulation is not always reflected in alumni financial support to HBCUs. Nationally, alumni giving rates hover around 20 percent and that number drops to 9 percent at HBCUs (Cohen, 2006; Cohen, 2008; Gasman & Anderson-Thompkins, 2003).

There are several reasons for these lower rates, but none of them should be used as an excuse for not giving. First, it takes money to make money, and as we have noted, many HBCUs (not all) have small fundraising infrastructures and insufficient funds to aggressively go after alumni dollars. If you don't ask, you don't receive. According to Ayers & Associates (2002), the average institutional advancement and alumni affairs budgets are lower at HBCUs than at majority institutions. Likewise, the average number of professional and support staff is lower at HBCUs compared to their majority counterparts, with majority institutions typically having double the professional staff and nearly double the support staff (Ayers & Associates, 2002). Second, African Americans have less access to wealth in the United States. For example, the median assets for a White family in the country are roughly $88,000 whereas for a Black family they are a mere $5,800 (Gasman & Sedgwick, 2005; Lui, Robles, & Leondar-Wright, 2005). Regardless, when compared with their White counterparts, African Americans give more of their discretionary income to charity (Gasman & Sedgwick, 2005). They are motivated to give by efforts to advance racial uplift in Black communities, out of a sense of obligation, as a result of peer and family influence, and by concrete, visible results (Gasman &

Anderson-Thompkins, 2003; Gasman & Sedgwick, 2005). And, in 2009, not only did African Americans have $900 billion in buying power, but their investment in the stock market was up by 30 percent (Flyin' West Marketing, 2011). Third, some alumni of public HBCUs are under the impression that the state fully funds their alma mater (an impression held by alumni of public HWIs as well). The truth is that most public HBCUs do not receive anywhere near enough funds from the state to educate their students.

Often when HBCUs are facing a crisis, alumni come home and support their alma maters. This is noble, but it is not enough and reinforces a survival mentality. Alumni must give on a regular basis—changing the HBCU mentality from survive to thrive as the White House Director on HBCUs, John S. Wilson, recently stated. Consistent giving along the same lines as tithing to the church or paying the cable bill is what is needed to support HBCUs and raise them to new levels.

An obvious question surfaces when discussing HBCU alumni giving, "Why wouldn't someone want to support the institution that gave them their start?" and more importantly, "Why should anyone else want to support this institution if alumni do not?" These days as outside groups, such as foundations and corporations, are becoming stricter with their funding priorities, they are asking these questions and rightfully so. Some funders are of the mindset that a college or university needs to have internal support before asking outsiders for funds.

Would increased alumni giving make a difference within the HBCU context? Consider this, if each of the 105 HBCUs secured a $500 donation annually for five years from 5000 of their alumni, it would yield over $1.3 billion or $12.5 million per school. In some cases, alumni need to be reminded of the value of their education and to be asked "Where would you be without your HBCU degree?"

Many HBCUs have not been diligent about remaining in

contact with their alumni over the years (Hunter, Jones, & Boger, 1999). As a result, the initial strategies for engaging alumni support must be done with care. Deciding on appropriate approaches that will re-introduce alumni to the challenges of the institution as well as define their expected roles can prevent a confused and misunderstood message. Reaching out to alumni, even if an institution has failed to do so in the past, provides an opportunity to educate alumni on the HBCU's needs. In addition, these efforts demonstrate that the HBCU still cares about the perspectives of alumni (Wunnava & Lauze, 2000). Alumni appreciate it when the institution asks about their concerns and are even more responsive when answers to these concerns are provided (Hunter, Jones, & Boger, 1999; Holmes, 2009).

AFRICAN AMERICAN ALUMNI MOTIVATIONS FOR GIVING

One of the most obvious, but most overlooked motivations for giving among African Americans is being asked to give. Oftentimes Blacks are assumed to be recipients of giving only—even within the HBCU context. For too long, many HBCUs have neglected to ask their alumni to give and support their alma maters.

Reaching out to alumni requires an understanding of African American motivations for giving and what kinds of appeals work best in terms of tapping into those motivations. First and foremost, appeals to alumni should be focused on racial uplift. Those at HBCUs know this inherently but they are not using this knowledge to cultivate and solicit their alumni. By and large, African American alumni are motivated to engage and to give by a sense of urgency around uplifting the Black race. They feel a sense of obligation and responsibility to pay their education forward. Demonstrating the concrete ways that alumni contributions will shape the lives of other African Americans is essential.

This sense of uplifting the Black race can also be seen in African Americans that fully grasp the concept of paying education forward although they themselves may have never advanced beyond high school. For example, recently an HBCU development officer received a call from an individual who wanted to make a six-figure gift to the school as well as another HBCU in the same city. The potential supporter explained that although he never attended college, it had always been his life's dream to give such that others could achieve. As the conversation progressed, the development officer gathered the normal pertinent information and then decided to invite the individual to campus for a tour and to meet faculty and staff. However, to the development officer's surprise, the donor initially said "no," citing his lack of education and how inadequate that would make him feel, especially around strangers. At that point the development officer realized the true magnitude of this person's offering and sought to reassure him that his lack of education in no way compares to what is in his heart and his compassion.

Finally the donor accepted the invitation and a few months later, arrived on campus. Following a tour, a meeting with top level administrators, and some lunch, the donor and the development officer sat down to debrief. After admitting that this had been one of the best days of his life, the donor explained that while he had been on a college campus before, no one had ever stopped to talk to him. At this point, he decided to double the size of his gift.

Black alumni respond well to personal interaction as typically direct mail does not resonate with them in any substantial way. They want to be engaged and involved in hands-on ways that demonstrate their value to the institution. Building relationships with Black alumni leads to enhanced trust and as a result increased giving. Building trust among HBCU alumni is crucial as some had positive academic experiences, but were not pleased with the service they received in the student services area (as mentioned in the previous chapter). As personal attention builds trust and rebuilds relationships that may have been strained in the past, this may prove to be unrealistic given the limited recourses many HBCUs currently have however, touching each alumni must remain as a long-term goal .

Engaging HBCU alumni through their church membership is also a constructive way to reach potential donors. As research tells us, African Americans are heavily influenced by their churches and their respective ministers. Working with local churches to engage HBCU alumni who are members can be fruitful. In order to establish a good relationship with the church's minister and his or her congregants, it is vital for the HBCU to demonstrate its impact on the local community and its commitment to aiding the congregants in their continued education (Holloman, Gasman, & Anderson-Thompkins, 2003).

Black alumni are also motivated to give by their peers and by positive peer pressure in their friend circles and social-service organizations. Although we will talk more about this motivation and influence in the chapter on affinity groups, it is important to mention here that encouraging giving in 'giving circles' or among close friends among Black alumni is effective. Keeping these basic motivations in mind while reading this chapter on alumni engagement and giving will serve as a foundation for understanding our recommendations.

PASSIVE AND ACTIVE ENGAGEMENT

When it comes to engaging HBCU alumni there are both passive and active ways to proceed. Passive engagement involves educating, informing, and gathering information from alumni, whereas active engagement involves hands-on interaction with alumni and including them in the important work of the institution. It is necessary and productive to educate alumni on a consistent basis. Effective ways of educating include the distribution of newsletters and annual reports. Through these venues, alumni can become aware of institutional initiatives and programs, prominent students and faculty, fundraising updates, and institutional goals.

Some passive forms of engagement gather much needed information. Surveying alumni about their needs and perspectives tells them that their opinion matters. It is important to find out how alumni perceive the institution and its efforts to raise money and engage them. Surveying alumni can also serve as a venue for getting feedback on new ideas. Engaging questions might include why an alumnus gave or did not give to a recent campaign or the annual fund or how would they might like the institution to communicate with them. Answers to these questions give the advancement staff an idea of the effectiveness of their performance and strategies. In addition, they know what type of approach to use in the future.

Recently, at Prairie View A&M University, the advancement staff surveyed the alumni, asking why they did not give to the most recent capital campaign. Most alumni who didn't give responded that they were not asked. This response is consistent with literature on fundraising that shows the people do not give when they are not asked (Gasman & Anderson-Thompkins, 2003). Eighty-four percent of those alumni who responded to the PVAMU survey said that they would be willing to support their alma mater using their time, talent, and financial resources. Other findings included a willingness to support a future annual fund, to engage in more volunteer opportunities, and to be contacted more frequently. The survey taught the Prairie View advancement staff that they were under-utilizing their alumni and not taking advantage of the stakeholders that have had the most vested interests in the institution.

In addition to passive engagement, active engagement takes alumni relationships to a higher level (Willemain et al., 1994). One strategy is to hold alumni trainings, which emphasize reconnecting with the HBCU, asking for their assistance in reaching out to other alumni, and giving back to the institution. Organizations, such as the Thurgood Marshall College Fund (TMCF) and the United Negro College Fund (UNCF) have provided training to their member schools on individual HBCU campuses and at national conferences that focus on engaging alumni. The TMCF initiative, in partnership with the Lilly Endowment, Inc., offered matching grants to its member schools to further enhance their development capacity by increasing alumni participation in the fundraising process. The initiative featured a one-day training workshop conducted by Indiana University's Center on Philanthropy, which focused on maintaining contact with graduates, emphasizing the importance of giving back, and increasing alumni giving. Some HBCUs have taken advantage of these opportunities, including Prairie View A&M University, Texas Southern University, Claflin University, Xavier University of Louisiana, and Savannah State University.

In Prairie View's case, the institution learned a significant amount from participation in these alumni trainings. For example, the Prairie View staff was able to assess its effectiveness in the area of communication with alumni and to make changes based on this assessment. They learned that some of their alumni were confused by the various fundraising processes that take place simultaneously on their campus. They also learned that their alumni appreciate being communicated with regularly, including updates, rather than mere solicitations.

Research shows that engaging volunteers in meaningful tasks that will in turn enhance the organization usually results in greater volunteer commitments up to and including financial support (Weerts & Ronca, 2007; Harrison, 1994). One innovative strategy is the use of institutional ambassadors. These are HBCU alumni who work with those in enrollment management to recruit students for the institutions. They are equipped with information on the HBCU that they can share with potential students. These alumni attend college fairs, visit high schools, and coordinate campus tours for prospective students. If an institution uses these ambassadors to assist with the work of the HBCU, it must make sure the ambassadors are equipped with the necessary publications, equipment, and tools to properly represent the institution otherwise alumni will become frustrated and disengaged.

Once an alumnus becomes comfortable representing the institution in an official capacity, and if they want to become more involved, they can be moved to a new level of commitment. One example of this higher level of commitment is a fundraising ambassador. These individuals must have a previous financial commitment to the HBCU. They must also agree to cultivate and solicit fellow alumni who have been identified as having a willingness and capacity to give. It is important to spend ample time training fundraising ambassadors prior to asking them to solicit donors. They need to be aware of the specific rules and regulations around the issue of fundraising. It is also necessary to keep a tighter reign on those individuals raising funds, ensuring that they properly represent the HBCU.

NATIONAL ALUMNI ASSOCIATIONS

The first alumni association was created at Williams College in 1821. Since then alumni have been coming together in support of their alma maters at colleges and universities across the country. Early alumni associations merely maintained mailing lists of alumni, collected dues, and produced periodic publications. Over time, alumni association became more active and, in fact, alumni were the first fundraisers of colleges and universities with some alumni organizing capital campaigns. Although barely mentioned today, the fundraising profession has its roots in alumni relations. Fundraisers are the result of institutions needing to reach out to a broader constituency than their alumni. In order to do so, colleges and universities needed professionals on staff. Of note, the professionalization of fundraisers has resulted in the decline of the relative importance of alumni associations.

There are three types of alumni associations. There are those that are independent of the institution of higher education. They govern themselves completely and receive no institutional funding. There are those that are interdependent, with the president reporting to the association and the institution. And, there are those that are dependent and are actualized in the form of a department that receives its funding from the institution (Cohen, 2008).

Depending on the college or university, an alumni association might be funded differently. Private institutions have a stronger history of supporting alumni activities as they are looking for long-term financial support from their alumni. Public colleges and universities often ask their alumni associations to find additional revenue to support their programs and initiatives so that the institution can use institutional resources to serve current students. Most alumni associations secure funding either from the college or university with which they are affiliated, the institution's foundation, membership dues, or sponsored programs.

Alumni association board members are of two types. The first type consists of 'influencers' and these individuals exert power and prestige. They have contacts or relationships that can assist the institution in advancing its goals. The second type consists of 'representatives' and these individuals have a history of involvement with the association and are elected to the alumni board in recognition of their loyalty and service.

Research tells us that membership in HBCU alumni association has decreased in the past three decades (Cohen, 2008). Alumni are not convinced that membership has benefits. According to Cohen (2008), "Unlike the former generations who reached out with an appeal of 'give until it hurts,' this new breed of alumni will need to see the personal and practical benefit of supporting alma mater" (p. 32). In reality, the typical HBCU and its affiliate alumni association have a rocky and somewhat disjointed relationship. Very often a slight difference of opinion such as the university insisting on reviewing financial records and the association being adamant about their autonomy can lead to years of separation and irreparable damage. This can prove disastrous for both sides as the outside public and alumni wanting to re-engage typically will assume that the university and the alumni association are intertwined and act as one. The usual path to reconnect to an HBCU is to contact the alumni relations office first. However, if the relationship between this office and the national alumni association is unhealthy, it is unlikely that a referral will be made.

There are several concrete ways that HBCUs can enhance their relationships with their national alumni associations (NAA). First, the college or university can invite members of the NAA to serve as ex-officio members of various university committees, including those related to the capital campaign, annual galas, homecoming, and administrative and faculty searches. This kind of gesture sends alumni a clear message that their opinion matters and that they are valued.

Next, to provide opportunities for even greater hands-on involvement by members of the NAA, the institution can involve them on admissions teams that reach out to prospective students. NAA members, who are typically active in local and national circles, are also excellent resources for students seeking future employment. The career services staff should enlist their efforts. And, as many NAA members are politically active, having them advocate on behalf of the college or university at all levels of government is advantageous.

Another approach to engaging the NAA is for the college or university to play an active role in the activities of the NAA itself. For example, participating in NAA-sponsored fundraising events, membership drives, and annual conventions demonstrates the institution's commitment to the success of its affiliate organization and values the work of the NAA.

One simple solution that alumni associations should consider is developing an alumni association handbook. This effort would reduce and potentially eliminate the confusion that often leads to unhealthy relations between the association and the school. This "How To Guide" would clearly define the purpose, functionality, and inter-workings of the national alumni associations such that the gray areas would be removed. Savannah State University's National Alumni Association has such a manual that provides information on the organizational structure, constitution, and by-laws and serves as a resource for graduates and supporters of the institution. The motive for creating such a standardized document centered on establishing a degree of uniformity of procedures among the regional alumni chapters, affiliates, and the university.

YOUNG ALUMNI ASSOCIATIONS

Often young alumni find it difficult to relate to the interests of older alumni due to generational differences. Rather than trying to cater to the vast needs of all alumni, some HBCUs are allowing young alumni to form their own organizations, while also joining the national alumni association. Although there can be some resistance to the forming of separate groups, catering to young alumni who have a lot of energy is advantageous to the institution. At Benedict College, for example, the national alumni association initially did not like the idea of a young alumni association, but eventually embraced it. Benedict's institutional advancement office, under the leadership of Love Collins, supported the young alumni, paying for a retreat and for speakers to talk with the group. The young alumni group was seeking the best strategies for engaging other young alumni in their efforts.

Often fundraisers think that the same strategies work with all alumni, but just as race and gender play a part in engagement and fundraising strategies, so does age (Walton & Gasman, 2008). Young alumni respond much better to face-to-face asks and when they are highly involved in their alma mater. They also are more likely to give if they have a social connection to the person asking. Rather than giving to abstract ideas, such as an endowment, young alumni tend to give to specific projects—especially those projects that have the potential for great change. They are looking for long-term impact and want to be kept informed of any actions that result from their generosity. Young alumni are also craving a voice at their alma mater and a leadership role (Drezner, 2010).

One of the main differences between younger and older alumni is young alumni's inclination toward social media. Rather than traditional brochures and direct mail, young alumni respond to solicitations and engagement efforts via social networking. As they are willing to ask others to join them in giving, social networking is an effective way to solicit friends on behalf of their alma mater. We want to emphasize the importance of being open to social media with young people (and the growing number of older alumni). Too many administrators are resistant to using social media and this resistance leads to a decrease in the bottom line when it comes to engaging young alumni and their potential donations. Young alumni are less apt to use email and snail mail and instead rely on Facebook messages, Twitter, and texting. Administrators need to pay attention to changing technology and engage alumni in the ways that resonate most with them.

There are a number of ways to involve young alumni association members on campus. First, invitations back to campus to speak to students are effective. These invitations not only offer a compliment to young alumni, but their presence can act as a source of inspiration to students as the success of these young people seems more attainable. Young alumni tend to be socially conscious and active. Having them speak about their experiences and the lessons they learned from their alma mater is an effective way to engage and keep young alumni engaged at a high level.

If an HBCU decides to have a young alumni association, it is important to create formal lines of communication with the national alumni association. Having a meaningful bond between the two organizations is vital. In addition, young alumni can learn significantly from more seasoned alumni and vice versa. Older alumni can benefit from the energy of young alumni as well as learn new ways of engaging more alumni in the work of the alumni association. Younger alumni can learn about the history and legacy of alumni involvement in the HBCU. Affiliate organizations such as National Alumni Associations have a long-standing history of being advocates to the outside world for the HBCU, building strong group support far away from where the campus is located. Instilling this history in young alumni is vital to telling the story of the HBCU.

If an HBCU has a pre-advancement or pre-alumni organization, it is advantageous to build a bridge between the young alumni association and these organizations as well. More than likely the future membership of the young alumni group will be made up of active former students and getting them acclimated early is never a bad idea. Young alumni model future success for student groups. Typically, when students graduate, they are consumed with starting their adult lives and careers and having a connection to their alma mater is not front and center in their minds. A relationship with the young alumni association can keep these new graduates involved and aware of opportunities and their role as alumni.

CREATING FUTURE ALUMNI

As noted, the alumni giving percentages at HBCUs are low. One way to combat these low rates is to engage and educate students while they are on campus. Most HBCUs fail to reach out to African Americans when they are students. According to Jim Anderson, "We start talking to students about giving in their freshmen orientation and in the freshmen curriculum. We remind them throughout the freshman year seminars and then in any other gatherings that we have through the year." In fact, at Fayetteville State, the student leaders have taken a formal approach to fundraising. The student government association takes the message of giving back to the students in a variety of venues.

There are numerous opportunities in which to involve future alumni and it is essential that students learn about giving back and continuing the legacy of education for others—the moment they step onto campus. One HBCU alumnus shared a story about being introduced to the concept of giving early on and 26 years later, he still does:

During freshman orientation week, we (freshman) had gone through the checklist of do's and don'ts, history of the school and surviving college rhetoric—needless to say, by week's end, we were thoroughly informed. However, on the final day, a member of the alumni association came and spoke about our future responsibility as graduates. Initially, I found that to be a bit strange since his speech seemed about four years pre-mature but toward the end of his message, he made a statement that helped shape my college experience. He said, 'this institution is known for producing thousands and thousands of graduates over the last one hundred years but, our alumni numbers only reflect a small percentage of this. The difference is, graduates get-it and go, while alumni get-it and give back ... which one are you going to be?

Students may not be able to give large sums of money initially, but getting people in the habit of donating their time and talent is essential. It also makes these students feel more a part of the institution. A good example in this area is the United Negro College Fund's (UNCF) Pre-Alumni Council. The Pre-Alumni Councils at individual UNCF schools raise considerable money from students each year and cultivate the notion of giving among the students involved. Of note, programs aimed at bringing students into the fundraising process need to include an educational component so that students begin to understand why giving monetarily is so important to the future success of their HBCU.

HBCUs can also start collegiate chapters of the Association of Fundraising Professionals (AFP) in an effort to engage students in fundraising. The AFP Collegiate Chapter Program was designed to educate undergraduate and graduate students about philanthropy and its significance to the good of mankind as well as to inform young people on the various career options available in fundraising profession. The chapter is formed on a college or university campus and is linked with a professional AFP chapter in the geographic area for mentoring and guidance. As typical of student organizations on college campuses, the chapter will have a faculty and staff advisor from the institution. In order to have a successful AFP collegiate chapter, it is important to involve student leaders who have experience working with similar organizations on campus or those who have raised funds for their student organizations.

Another avenue for planting the giving seed within the student body as well as gaining assistance with extending the university's "giving message" through campus is to utilize the talents of students as callers. Many institutions conduct phon-a-thons as a method of fundraising for the annual fund as well as establishing bonds between former and current students. During our research for this book, we discovered countless examples of connections being established between the past and present that had a lasting influence on the students.

There was one student who helped an alumnus secure a commencement program from his graduation ceremony more than 40 years ago. And another instance where the student used her own money to send an elderly alumna a university tee shirt. "I just wanted to help in any way I could," said the student. Creating this sense of bonding with former graduates helps to educate future alumni on what being an alumnus really means and more importantly, what it means to give back.

Often through this brief experience with fundraising, these phon-a-thoners amass enough of an understanding and practical exposure to philanthropy to assist the development office in creating more of a culture of philanthropy on campus. Another advantage—this captive audience is an ideal and inexpensive workforce that will pay dividends for generations to come.

NATIONAL EFFORTS TO INCREASE FUNDRAISING AND ALUMNI GIVING

The importance of fundraising, especially alumni giving, at HBCUs has been recognized by several national organizations and foundations. For example, in 1999, the Kresge Foundation, along with the Southern Education Foundation (SEF), acknowledged that many HBCUs have limited financial resources for institutional advancement and for sophisticated fundraising efforts. Knowing that a strong advancement operation is vitally important to institution building, the grant-funded Kresge HBCU Initiative was created. Each institution of the five HBCUs that were supported by the grant (Bethune-Cookman College, Dillard University, Xavier University of Louisiana, Johnson C. Smith University, and Meharry Medical College) received a grant of roughly $2 million over a five-year period. The grants were focused on enhancing staffing, technology, and programming. With these added resources, the schools concentrated on raising new levels of support from alumni. This five-year program, which began in 2000, also made one-time grants to seven other HBCUs. The funder built in incentives throughout the grant process, offering up to $25,000 a year to institutions that made their annual benchmarks. In addition to monetary funding, the grantees were provided with professional consultants, mentoring, and shadowing opportunities for staff.

The institutions that participated in the Kresge HBCU Initiative were able to strengthen their fundraising areas and as a result their overall institutions. In addition, the Kresge Foundation sought to reduce HBCUs' reliance on federal funding programs and to bolster the abilities of HBCU leaders. This kind of infrastructure program is essential for HBCUs as it infuses money into an area of campus that helps to build the rest of the institution (Schultz, 2005).

The United Negro College Fund has also created a comprehensive program to support alumni giving and fundraising in addition to several other areas of its private HBCU members. The Institute for Capacity Building (ICB), which has been funded by the Mellon Foundation, focuses on strengthening the overall capacity of HBCUs. Although the initiative focuses on retention, degree completion, teaching and learning, and fiscal management, one of the main thrusts is fundraising. The ICB's HBCU Institutional Advancement Program, which began in 2008, has a particular focus on increasing alumni and trustee giving. UNCF member institutions can receive grants between $600,000–$1,000,000, customized technical assistance, professional development, and consultant expertise. The institutions that have received grants include: Bennett College for Women, Huston-Tillotson University, Talladega College, Virginia Union University, Claflin University, Philander Smith College, Wiley College, Benedict College, Jarvis Christian College, Morehouse College, and Fisk University. Of note, the first four HBCUs that participated in ICB's initiative (Bennett, Huston-Tillostson, Talladega, and Virginia Union) have demonstrated an average increase in alumni giving of 78 percent, an average increase in alumni participation of 68 percent, a 46 percent increase in unrestricted funding, and at least 90 percent board giving. Moreover, the four institutions located over 3500 lost alumni by enhancing their database systems.

All HBCUs, including public ones, could benefit greatly from more ICB-like initiatives. According to Shannon Fleming at Philander Smith College,

> the most important thing to move us along in the area of fundraising in the past three years has been our ICB grant from the UNCF. It allowed us to hire three more positions in institutional advancement and gave us the resources and operating funds we needed. This grant is one reason we have gone from 4 percent alumni giving to 12 percent and our board giving has increased from 30 percent to 40 percent. The grant allows us to push our board to give more. Our goal is 100 percent.

Robert Franklin, the president of Morehouse College, also described the importance and impact of a grant from the UNCF's ICB initiative. Morehouse received $900,000 and that funding enabled them to add four staff positions. He has seen measurable results, and, according to Franklin,

> When I arrived at the institution, the alumni giving was only 16 percent, in my second year it rose to 18 percent, in my third year it rose to 22 percent and this year we have really made an impact and are up to 39 percent.

Franklin also noted that his goal is to get the alumni giving percentage to 50 percent and be an inspiration to other HBCUs.

ANNUAL FUNDS

A rigorous annual fund campaign is essential to an increase in alumni giving and also enhances alumni engagement. Unlike a capital campaign, which is an intensive fundraising effort with specific goals, time frames, and funding designations, the annual fund is a yearly appeal designed to eventually garner the financial support of every member of the alumni. It is the foundation of any ongoing and healthy development program. Traditionally comprised of unrestricted gifts that are used for operations, the most valuable annual gifts can be defined as spendable, renewable, and upgradeable. Through a process sometimes referred to as donor mining, the institution, by appealing to the masses, hopes this will lead to more actual dollars and a larger pool of supporters. One need only review the approach the Obama campaign took in 2008, which resulted in a significant increase in supporters and dollars through an appeal to the masses. Another benefit of the annual fund is that it brings to the surface larger capacity donors that may not have been identified as such and who may have wanted to remain undetected.

Without an annual campaign, an organization often finds itself involved in crisis fundraising, which is also known as "Give us money or we will have to drop the program, go out of business, or fail to provide for people who need us—and it's going to be your fault!" According to Schultz (2005), in the Kresge Foundation report *Changing the Odds*, "The histories of HBCUs are filled with stories of presidents visiting wealthy philanthropists to request an urgent gift to 'save the institution'" (p. 15). However, by designing a fundraising program that is built around an annual campaign, this will not be the case. Instead there will be a carefully thought out, planned, and implemented approach to raising necessary money in an orderly and timely manner.

Two important things are derived from the annual fund. First, it assesses the validity and accuracy of the constituent based data.

Simply tallying the number of returned mailers, undeliverable emails, and incorrect phone numbers will give the organization a clearer view of the reliability of the database going forward. It also identifies a future volunteer pool that can be engaged in campus projects and fundraising campaigns and, as mentioned earlier in this section, it brings to the surface new donors.

Armed with the names of new donors, the advancement staff, for example, can perform segmented analysis on the top level donors. This strategy will help determine the appropriate strategy of solicitation. In addition, this approach will streamline the work of the development staff, identifying those alumni who should be cultivated and eventually solicited in a face-to-face visit. For example, at Prairie View A&M University, after the completion of a successful phon-a-thon, the advancement staff looked at all of the donors who contributed $100 or more. They conducted a wealth screening to determine what their actual giving capacity was and discovered that among the roughly 65 donors who had given at this level there was a giving potential of $6 million combined.

Overall, positive alumni relations leads to a stronger HBCU. If alumni are more engaged and happier with their alma mater, they are not only more likely to give financially but more eager to act as free publicity on behalf of the college or university. Having institutional ambassadors, formal or informal, is advantageous to the sustainability and livelihood of the institution.

Practical Recommendations

- Educate alumni about the overall needs of the institution and the importance of giving so that they are regular givers rather than "crisis" givers.
- Take advantage of all opportunities to enhance the skills of alumni relations and fundraising staff; investing in them is an investment in the future of the HBCU.

- Tie alumni appeals to a "sense of obligation" and "sense of racial uplift," giving alumni a sense of the role that they can and should play at the institution.
- Design alumni events and activities that build trust between alumni and the institution and among various alumni groups.
- Engage local churches with large numbers of alumni in the congregations, sharing stories of student as well as institutional success.
- Build peer-to-peer alumni networks to encourage fundraising and connections with the institution.
- Ask the opinion of alumni through focus groups and surveys and digest their suggestions in an effort to improve the HBCU.
- Engage alumni donors as institutional ambassadors who represent the institution throughout the country and locally.
- Work diligently to build strong relationships with the National Alumni Association as any appearance of infighting appears as chaos to outsiders, especially funders. They want to see everyone on the same page in terms of institutional support.
- Consider affinity groups within alumni associations to speak to generational gaps among alumni. Alumni's preferences in terms of social interaction and giving tend to differ depending on age.
- Create future alumni by educating current students about the value of giving back and the necessity of fundraising.

5

ENGAGING AFFINITY GROUPS

Among the many supporters of HBCUs are the various affinity groups affiliated with the institutions. These include classes, fraternities and sororities, marching band alumni, student leaders, and local and national social service organizations. Oftentimes, HBCUs do not capitalize on these affinity groups, many of which have affluent and influential members. In this chapter we explore the potential for engaging and raising funds from these groups.

CLASS ENGAGEMENT AND CLASS GIFTS

Some of the most obvious affinity groups that can enhance institutional giving are individual "classes" of the college or university. Alumni have an allegiance to the year that they graduated and to those who graduated with them. Alumni look forward to the anniversary of their graduation year. Bringing these graduates back to campus at regular intervals, such as every five and ten years, can solidify their engagement with the HBCU and also enhance giving. Moreover, this type of engagement often culminates with the 50th reunion and a significant class gift.

One example of this culmination is the "Golden Anniversary Class" at Prairie View A&M University. Each year, graduates celebrating their 50th class reunion have in most cases made a six-figure gift to the institution. Roughly five years prior to their 50th reunion, alumni begin to plan and organize; starting with contacting the university to secure names and addresses of classmates. The 50th reunion planning group meets regularly, establishes fundraising goals, and plans many fundraising events. These activities lead up to homecoming during their reunion year and result in a gift ranging from $100,000–$200,000.

Of significance are the events that the 50th reunion planning group sponsors during the five-year period prior to their reunion. These events are aimed at engaging alumni who may have lost touch or not been on campus for years. One event includes adopting an incoming class of freshmen whose graduation date coincides with their 50th reunion. Adoption starts at freshmen orientation with alumni providing an overview of the four-year partnership to the students. Adoption means that the 50th reunion alumni mentor the students in the freshmen class, offering career advice, building relationships for students with the National Alumni Association, and providing scholarships. The relationships between alumni and freshmen are facilitated by the University College administration. University College is a freshmen neighborhood that provides a living and learning environment to support academic success and helps students make the transition to college.

The key to bringing alumni together for their 50th reunion and securing a substantial institutional gift is to engage them at regular intervals throughout their lives. This engagement can be focused on homecoming, founder's day, or any significant occasion that the institution celebrates.

FRATERNITIES AND SORORITIES

In addition to individual classes, which are a natural affinity group to any institution, fraternities and sororities are a potential source of engaged and active alumni. As those in the HBCU community know well, many students are active in fraternities and sororities. Research tells us that members of African American fraternities and sororities typically remain active throughout their lifetimes and are heavily influenced by the actions of their peers (Brown, Parks, & Phillips, 2010; Kimbrough, 2003; Ross, 2001). Because of the long-term friendships and the sense of obligation among fraternity and sorority members, they are an important group to engage in the fundraising process. Of note, Black fraternities and sororities are significantly different from those of their White counterparts. White Greek organizations, while maintaining a national presence, do not have active adult membership and, as such, do not serve as affinity groups at majority institutions.

Not only do Black Greek organizational members have ties with those current students on campus, they keep in touch with one another long after graduation. In addition, many fraternity and sorority members are quite successful and have discretionary income that could be donated to HBCUs. Development officers should engage the more prominent members of these groups and ask them to present the cause of an HBCU education at fraternity and sorority gatherings and formal events. These leaders have much influence over their peers and can be effective in conveying a profound message about the influence of the HBCU. Messages of racial uplift and providing opportunities to a future generation are powerful ways of engaging members of fraternities and sororities.

Another effective approach is to invite members of nearby Black Greek organizations to work with student programs on campus. By doing this, they are reunited with many of the positive experiences of their alma mater and more likely to want to give back as a result. They will also be more acutely aware of the needs on campus if they are on the campus and more likely to talk about those needs with fellow fraternity and sorority members.

Once the Black Greek members are engaged, encouraging them to participate in giving circles can be advantageous. For example, an HBCU can establish giving circles with the Alphas and the Kappas, encouraging some healthy competition among these groups. The same can be done with the AKAs and the Deltas. The beauty of this kind of competition is that there is already rivalry among these organizations. Capturing this rivalry and using it to benefit the HBCU is an innovative way to raise funds.

MARCHING BAND ALUMNI

According to a 2007 article in *The New York Times*, the marching band at an HBCU is more than just a band. George Edwards, who directed the marching band at Prairie View A&M University, explained that playing in the marching band leads to increased success in school. Students are required to maintain a minimum grade point average to receive band scholarships, which can certainly help to offset college costs. Moreover, he noted that being a member of a marching band can have the feel of a family, especially on more isolated campuses (Ratliff, 2007).

This "family" relationship is ideal for cultivating a high level connection between marching band members and the HBCU. When reaching out to alumni, development officers should draw upon the experiences that many students had in the marching band. Moreover, when band members graduate, the development office should keep in touch with these individuals, flagging them as having potential to come back to campus to work with current marching band members and having the kind of connection that could result in a financial donation.

STUDENT LEADERS

Student leaders are the most engaged students on college campuses. HBCUs have countless young people working on programming boards, in student government, with homecoming activities, and in the residence halls. These individuals have strong ties to the institution, which can be capitalized on once they are alumni. Not only are these active student leaders easier to engage and bring into the alumni family, but they are comfortable motivating others. Current student leaders can help an advancement office keep in touch with former student leaders.

Affinity groups can be set up around the particular type of student leadership in which the student was involved. For example, oftentimes those who were on the homecoming committee as students want to be leaders during alumni homecoming events. They have a great deal of experience and have positive relationships with their peers. Likewise, those students involved in student government often want to serve as class representatives. They tend to be leaders and well-organized individuals, possessing skills that are necessary for assistance with class gift drives. Regardless of the specific leadership role while on campus, student leaders are primed to be molded into alumni leaders.

LOCAL AND NATIONAL SOCIAL SERVICE ORGANIZATIONS

The last major affinity group that can be instrumental to increasing alumni and donor giving is those social and service organizations affiliated with African Americans. These groups include the Links, Inc., the Boule, 100 Black Men, as well as other fraternal organizations. Whether the members of these groups are alumni or not they can be tapped for engagement on the HBCU campus. All of these organizations have long histories of raising scholarship monies and being actively involved with HBCUs. Far too often, however, they go untapped by those in institutional advancement. Much like fraternities and sororities, these social service organizations have leaders who hold a good amount of influence over their members. Leaders typically try to leave a mark on the organization and approaching these leaders with the idea of making an HBCU part of their agenda can result in significant contributions from members. For example, the Links, Inc. has established an HBCU Endowment Trust, raising over $300,000 for the trust in recent years. And most recently, the international organization gave $10,000 scholarships to Edward Waters College, Spelman College, Bennett College for Women, Bethune-Cookman College, and Florida Memorial University (www.linksinc.org).

We think it is important to point out that while the usual affinity groups are vitally important to fundraising success, developing institution-specific affinity groups is also important. By studying the institution's history and speaking with alumni about their most treasured traditions and memories, advancement officers can identify potential affinity groups. For instance, at Prairie View A&M University, Lauretta Byars, the vice president for Institutional Relations at the time, created a historical marker program that brought together alumni with an affinity toward particular buildings on campus, such as residence halls, the former campus center, and a hospital that was the birthplace for many of the former students.

Unfortunately, due to unequal funding, many of Prairie View's early buildings were not built to last and often made with substandard materials. As a result, quite a few of these buildings no longer exist and neither does the Prairie View campus of the past. For years, alumni had difficulty connecting with the newer look of the institution and their memories. The historical marker program provided an opportunity for alumni to re-live their time on campus by providing a walking tour, which highlights the institution's past and reconnects alumni to the university. Because specific alumni groups had affinities for particular buildings, the institutional advancement staff sought their financial support to secure a historical marker.

Many HBCUs do reach out to affinity groups but many do not. Instead they rely on corporate and foundation contributions. These affinity groups need to be cultivated and brought into the HBCU family. They need to be told the story of the HBCU's impact and shown their role in making a more substantial contribution to that impact.

Practical Recommendations

- Think about the unique affinity groups on your campus. What makes students come together while undergraduates and how can these affiliations spill over into their lives as alumni?
- Connect various on-campus affinity groups, such as individual classes, with current students to build memories and a sense of community.
- Capitalize on the positive peer pressure that exists within groups. This peer pressure can be used to influence members of adult chapters of fraternities and sororities as well as other organizations.
- Build upon the natural rivalry between campus groups. Although people have graduated, they still hold fast to rivalries developed in college. Competition can lead to increased giving if captured properly.
- Remember to transform student leaders into alumni leaders. The same skills that served these students well when they were on campus can serve the institution after they graduate.

6

CORPORATE AND FOUNDATION GIVING

Corporations and foundations have a long and complex history of providing support for institutions of higher education. Depending on societal factors, they have focused attention on higher education or looked away to other causes, such as worldwide disease or the arts. In the case of historically Black colleges and universities, corporations and foundations have a sordid past. In the late 1800s and early 1900s, industrial philanthropists, who owned the corporations and established most foundations, supported HBCUs but did so with considerable strings attached to this support. For the most part, they pushed industrial education, which emphasized manual labor, on African Americans. This push was based on their need for a semi-skilled labor class to work at their companies (Anderson, 1988). Black intellectuals at the time, including W.E.B. Du Bois, were heavily critical of the support of HBCUs by these industrial philanthropists, pointing to their ulterior motives.

Eventually, by the 1930s, corporate and foundation philanthropy shifted and the major philanthropists began to funnel money toward a classical arts curriculum (Anderson, 1988). However, there were still considerable strings attached, leading HBCU students to rise up and fight against some of the White HBCU presidents' draconian practices for stifling student speech and actions. These presidents were often seen as puppets of the philanthropists because they were dependent on the philanthropists' money.

These early relationships have shaped the interactions between HBCUs, corporations, and foundations and have led to suspicions on the part of HBCUs on occasion. In the current context, it is essential that HBCUs maintain their integrity when working with corporations and foundations. HBCUs need to set the agenda for their future and the needs of their students. Adhering to the institutional mission with a willingness to change in positive ways is imperative when working with corporations and foundations rather than merely acquiescing to their interests and agendas. When working with corporations, in particular, HBCUs need to make sure that the corporation's products and actions are not in disagreement with the goals of the institution.

APPROACHING FOUNDATIONS AND CORPORATIONS

There are two major mistakes that HBCUs make when approaching corporations and foundations for funding. As these happen over and over, we think it is important to state them upfront. First, it is essential that HBCUs increase their alumni giving before approaching outsiders to fund the institution. Foundations and corporations look at participation rates when deciding whether or not to make an investment in an institution. If those on the inside do not support the institution, it is quite difficult to get others to do so. For far too long, corporations and foundations have been the main funding source of HBCUs, but these entities cannot continue to be the major source of funding as more and more institutions are clamoring for their attention.

Second, HBCUs need to craft their approaches to corporations and foundations in terms of success rather than need. In the past, solicitations that were focused on need or even "neediness" resonated with corporations and foundations, but in the previous ten years much has changed in terms of grant making. These changes are a product of shifts in marketing and a focus on outcomes. The best example of this change in focus from "needy" to success-oriented can be seen in the marketing and promotion of the long-standing nonprofit organization CARE. In its earlier years CARE had ads that featured poor African children eating porridge and surrounded by flies. This same organization now boasts beautiful, full color ads that feature African girls and women with the words "I am powerful" underneath them. The ads are trying to convince us that women are the world's most plentiful natural resource. In the 21st Century, these ads resonate with individual donors, foundations, and corporations. HBCUs need to retool their approaches to be more success-oriented, focusing on the strengths that they possess.

In addition to focusing on success when approaching corporations and foundations, HBCUs need to identify and share their institutional niches. Those HBCUs that are most successful at securing funding are those that have easily identifiable niches and strengths. An institution's strengths need to be at the forefront of the funder's mind and be interesting and unique enough to stay there. For example, Xavier University of Louisiana is known among funders and the higher education community as an institution that disproportionately produces African American students who pursue degrees in medicine. It has a strong science undergraduate program that is bolstered with summer research opportunities (Perna et al., 2009). Likewise, Spelman College has a reputation for producing African American women who pursue degrees in the graduate sciences. It has a substantial track record that it has documented and shared for decades and this has resulted in funders looking their way (Perna et al., 2009). As mentioned earlier, under the leadership of Walter Kimbrough, Philander Smith College has adopted a social justice mission. Its motto "Think Justice" has enabled it to gain attention from funders, including the Kresge Foundation. When Kimbrough arrived at the small Little Rock campus it was not known for specific strengths and he wanted to change that, bolstering the reputation of the college.

Corporations and foundations are highly outcomes focused. They want to make sure that the institutions in which they invest money are stable. Not only do funders want to see supporting data when HBCUs apply for funding, but they want HBCUs to collect data that demonstrates the value of the funder's investment. Having an outcomes-oriented approach that is predicated on demonstrating your institution's success is essential to securing corporate and foundation support.

THE ROLE OF THE HBCUS

When reaching out to corporations and foundations there is much that HBCUs must do to ensure a positive and effective relationship with funders. It is important, for example, to pursue grant opportunities that fit with the institution's needs and goals. An HBCU does not want to chase after funding that does not complement its strengths. Not only is this a poor use of resources, but if the institution does not have enough expertise in the area, it can serve as a hindrance and a nuisance. The HBCU has to have the capacity to adhere to the grant requirements.

Once an HBCU secures a grant, it is vital that the administration learn to "manage up." The best thing that an HBCU can do is to consistently tell the funder how the money is being used and the success that is resulting from the donation. Funders like to be involved in the gifts they make. The worst thing than an HBCU can do after getting a grant is to remain quiet.

Although it may be obvious, another important aspect of securing a corporate or foundation grant is spending the money. When funders give, they want to see the money being used and want to know how an institution is spending the grant. When researching this book, we talked to one development officer who was very frustrated with a dean who had helped secure a major grant to fund faculty positions. The grant was wide-reaching and could have been a change agent in the science department for which it was secured; however, the dean of the college of arts and sciences did not spend the money and failed to launch a search for faculty after three years of having the grant. When the foundation learned of the lack of action on the part of the HBCU dean, they were disappointed and wanted to pull the funds. Perhaps what is most disturbing about this situation is that the foundation learned about the lack of spending when the dean approached it for additional funding for another project. There are several things wrong with this situation. First, the dean did not spend the money secured through the grant procurement process. And second, the dean approached a foundation for another grant, knowing that he had not used the first grant. This situation showed the HBCU in a bad light and the lack of spending sent a signal to the foundation that the HBCU did not need the money. Perhaps the worst result of the dean's actions is that the HBCU's reputation was sullied in the eyes of the foundation. This makes for a difficult situation as foundation personnel talk to each other and a mistake with one foundation can lead to a lack of support from multiple foundations. It is vital for HBCUs to manage their reputations.

The last bit of advice that we have for working with corporations and foundations is that it is important to realize that they are private entities that can give their money to whomever they want. It is important that the HBCU does not take funder relationships for granted, but instead nurtures these relationships to ensure future support.

Practical Recommendations

- It is important to properly manage funding relationships by "managing up." This means that you need to regularly tell your institutional story to your current and potential funders. The more funders know, the more they can make informed decisions about your institutional funding in the future and tell your story to others.
- Before approaching outside funders such as corporations and foundations, work to increase alumni giving at your institution. Funders want to see internal buy-in before supporting an institution.
- Focus your efforts on trumpeting the success of your institution rather than playing the violin. Funders want to invest in successful organizations.
- Manage all aspects of the grant or financial contribution with efficiency. The pathway to additional grant funding is paved with follow-through and open communication.
- Make sure to pursue grants and donations from foundations and corporations that have similar value systems to that of the HBCU. It is important not to merely chase money but to ensure than funding meets the needs of the institution.

7

BUILDING ENDOWMENTS

From Louisiana to West Virginia to North Carolina—and many states in between—a growing number of historically Black colleges and universities are coming off the sidelines and finally getting into the major fundraising game.

Reginald Stewart, 2011

Colleges and universities with stronger endowments are more stable financially, are more self-sufficient, and are able to generate revenue to support both new and existing programs and student scholarships. According to Spelman President Beverly Daniel Tatum, at her institution, "Successful fundraising efforts to increase the endowment provided financial stability and fueled construction of new residence halls and academic buildings—creating an attractive environment" for students. College and university endowment funds are designed to assist current and future generations of students, which means these funds need to stay steady regardless of inflation. However, what we have witnessed in recent years is a drastic decline in endowment values. According to the National Association of Colleges & University Business Officers (2010), the endowments of educational institutions went down 20 percent in 2009. This phenomenon has had a more substantial impact on HBCUs because their endowments are considerably lower than the majority of their historically White counterparts.

It's a fact. Endowments at HBCUs need to increase. Substantial efforts need to be directed toward enhancing endowments so that HBCUs have a firm foundation on which to operate. There are a number of reasons that HBCUs have had much smaller endowments then majority institutions. First, endowments build over time and due to past discrimination in funding at the state level, as well as within the foundation and corporate world, HBCU endowments have not grown at similar rates to their HWI counterparts (Gasman, 2010b). Second, public HBCUs, much like many of their HWI counterparts, have only in the past two decades reached out to their alumni, who had previously relied on ample state funding. However, times have changed and state funding has dried up quickly. Third, HBCUs have not traditionally focused on endowment building. Instead, they have paid attention to securing grants from corporations and foundations for infrastructure, physical plant expansion and enhancement, and scholarships. This chapter focuses on building endowments, including educating alumni on the value of institutional endowments, identifying areas of need and areas to enhance, determining feasibility, and championing success. It is not a "how to" chapter in the sense of building a basic endowment.

Currently the average endowment at a public HBCU is roughly $16 million whereas the average private HBCU endowment is roughly $25 million (IPEDS, 2009). If you pull the endowments of Spelman College ($351,700,000), Howard University ($338,440,000), Hampton University ($336,640,000), and Morehouse College ($128,900,000) out of the mix, the numbers drop substantially. According to a recent statistical report compiled by the United Negro College Fund's Frederick D. Patterson Research Institute, HBCUs (both public and private) have seen the values of their endowment assets increase steadily over the past six years. However, when compared to majority institutions, HBCUs have shown smaller gains (United Negro College Fund, 2011).

Enhancing HBCU endowments is vital in terms of keeping these institutions on stable ground, but more than that—healthy endowments ensure that HBCUs will thrive rather than merely survive. Moreover, strong endowments will help HBCUs to accomplish their goals and be more innovative. Lastly, a vigorous endowment cements the legacy of an institution, securing its future ability to educate students and contribute to society at large.

The information above is well-documented throughout the very limited research available on HBCU fundraising. So knowing this, why is it that the majority of HBCUs, privates as well as publics, have never attempted an endowment building campaign? Are they afraid of going after the big numbers—$20, $50, or $100 million coupled with the fear of failure? Many HBCUs have not had one; do not want to fail; are afraid of going after a big number; have not done a good assessment of overall need; do not have a goal or mission. Regardless of the reasons given, excuses for not building an endowment will only lead to a lack of stability among HBCUs and possibly the closure of more HBCUs.

ALUMNI EDUCATION

Research tells us that African Americans are much more likely to give to scholarship drives than they are to give to endowments

(Gasman & Anderson-Thompkins, 2003). The reason for this choice is that Blacks like to see concrete results from their giving. While African Americans give 60 percent of their discretionary income to the Church, this type of giving is very concrete. Churches rarely have endowments. As such, Blacks are used to giving to things they can see, such as building funds, choir robe funds, organ funds, etc. Of course, Blacks also tithe, which could appear to be abstract like endowment giving. However, as Blacks have been tithing for centuries and tithing has a direct connection to God and spirituality, it resonates differently than abstract endowments with African Americans. Often it is seen as an obligation and part of everyday life (Holloman et al., 2003).

Endowments, if not properly explained, can be somewhat nebulous. Despite this inclination to give toward more concrete initiatives, HBCUs can educate alumni in ways that change their minds about giving to endowments. One of the simplest ways to explain an endowment is to compare it to a savings account. We often tell alumni that the operating budget of the HBCU is similar to a household checking account. We use our checking accounts to pay day-to-day expenses and to sustain our basic daily life. However, we use our savings account to plan for the future and to make our dreams and those of our children and families come true. An endowment is the savings account of a college or university. It sustains the HBCU during difficult times, creates future success, and provides opportunity for those involved with the institution in the future.

According to Kathryn Miree (2003), a fundraising consultant, "One of the first stumbling blocks to building endowment is defining the term" (p. 3). When educating alumni on the importance of endowments, we need to communicate that endowments are long-term reserves for HBCUs. Unlike an annual gift or a scholarship gift, endowments are never spent, but rather stored away and invested for future growth. Year after year, these investments generate an interest return that the

institution uses to enhance existing programs, build new programs, support capital projects, and strengthen student services.
At first glance, this explanation seems very basic, but it is rarely
communicated to alumni. Instead, advancement staff members
often assume knowledge on the part of alumni. This assumption
has more than likely contributed to a lack of giving to an endowment on the part of alumni.

PLANNING FOR ENDOWMENT BUILDING

There are several steps necessary before beginning an endowment campaign. The first is to confront any internal challenges.
Staff members need to understand that building an endowment
is a team effort and the campus as a whole needs to understand
this role. Their role and their unique contributions need to be
made explicit prior to launching a campaign (Miree, 2003). In
the end, everyone on campus needs to be on board and have an
understanding of the task at hand.

Next, the HBCU needs to develop the maturity necessary to
lead a campaign. The institution should have an annual fund
so that the HBCU has a history of regular donors. The office of
institutional advancement needs to have all key positions filled
and the staff needs to understand its role in the campaign. Likewise, the board and president need to understand their roles and
responsibilities. It is important to convey that an "all campus
approach" is necessary.

Third, the HBCU needs to identify its areas of need and areas
that it hopes to build. It is important to involve both the administrative and academic side of the HBCU in determining the
needs of the institution. These individuals are involved with the
HBCU at the ground level and understand the day-to-day and
long-term needs of the institution. Typically, endowment campaigns include support for faculty endowed chairs, endowed
scholarships, student services support, a planned giving

endowment, school-specific needs, and support for technology and equipment.

Fourth, the HBCU needs to prepare a case statement that represents the needs of the institution but also makes a case for investment in the HBCU. It is designed to capture the specific role that the endowment will play in the future of the institution and should have a specified end date. According to Miree (2003), "The endowment case statement differs from the annual case statement since it focuses on future needs and resources" (p. 5). The case statement should also make it clear to potential donors that the HBCU has the skills and capability to be successful in its pursuit of endowment monies. Specifically, a case statement needs to develop the theme and set the tone for the campaign. It needs to pull the potential donor into the institution and make an emotional connection. Donors should be able to sense the role they can play in supporting the institution. The statement must convey a sense of need and urgency while also highlighting the contributions and success of the HBCU. In addition to discussing the current needs and role of the HBCU, the statement should describe the history and mission of the institution for those less familiar with it. Lastly, the case needs to detail what will be required to meet the needs of the institution and ultimately promote increased learning among the HBCU's students (Miree, 2003). Earlier in the chapter, we noted that African American alumni have not always grasped the necessity of building an endowment. However, it is vital to fully explain in the case statement how increasing the endowment will enhance the value of the alumni's degree as well as create a stronger institution for future generations.

DETERMINING FEASIBILITY

Another step that must be taken before initiating an endowment campaign is to determine the feasibility for conducting such a campaign. The HBCU needs to ask itself a series of questions. The first question should be: is the endowment goal realistic? Another question to ask is: are the institutional needs identified and included in the case statement wholly supported by those who were surveyed to determine the needs? Those needs that have across the board support are the most likely to be embraced by donors.

The next question is whether the HBCU has a sufficient donor base to support the financial goal? The HBCU must also ask itself if the board is significantly engaged with the institution and ready to make major gifts, including a portion of the lead gifts. Those capable of making lead gifts are likely those that have been annual fund donors consistently, have given major gifts, have led volunteer efforts, and perhaps have served on various institutional advisory boards (Miree, 2003). Likewise, the HBCU has to assess its volunteer base to determine if it has a cadre of volunteers that is eager to offer support for the campaign through both giving and asking others to give (Miree, 2003). It is also important for the institution to assess its technology and whether it has the ability to manage the endowment building process and whether its alumni data is reliable. Lastly, and of the utmost importance, the HBCU needs to determine if it has an individual with enough connections and charisma available to chair the campaign.

ROLES OF THE PRESIDENT AND THE BOARD

Although we have discussed the significant role of the president in fundraising earlier in this book, the president plays a particularly significant role in an endowment building campaign and needs to be prepared in advance for that role. The president serves as the main connector between the institution and the board of trustees and endowment campaign steering committee. He or she must be able to effectively communicate the long-term strategic goals of the institution and the long-term needs of the HBCU. The president must also have the knowledge and confidence to push for increased participation among board members.

Board members must demonstrate giving for other donors. They need to be intimately familiar with the needs and goals of the institution. In addition to giving a personal gift toward the endowment campaign, board members must also commit to identifying potential donors and securing additional gifts from these donors. The more personal involvement on the part of the board members the more potential success is within reach of the HBCU.

CAPTURING CAMPAIGN SUCCESS

During and after the campaign, it is vital to promote the HBCU's success. Donors and internal constituents need to be kept aware of milestones throughout the campaign as this encourages them to give more and promote giving among other alumni. Because African Americans prefer concrete forms of giving, providing information on the way the endowment monies are being used is essential. For example, if monies are used to support endowed scholarships and professorships, this information must be communicated to donors regularly. Reporting on endowment building success generates more enthusiasm for additional giving. Moreover, when donors and volunteers see the success of their efforts, their commitment to the institution increases and they have more ownership of the campaign. These internalized feelings lead to a desire to complete the campaign successfully (Miree, 2003).

Practical Recommendations

- Identify the institution's areas of need and its dreams before beginning the campaign.

- Confirm that the institution has a solid donor base on which to rely for both voluntary and monetary support.
- When building support for an endowment campaign, talk to donors about the institution's success.
- Educate alumni about the definition and purpose of an endowment so the concept is perfectly clear.
- Make sure that the president understands his or her role and is comfortable with the fundraising task ahead.
- Educate the board members on their role in a successful endowment campaign and ensure that a high percentage of the lead gifts come from this group of individuals.
- Promote the institution's success to donors and the media during and after the endowment campaign. This strategy will engender enthusiasm and spread the institution's success beyond the walls of the campus.

8

TELLING A BETTER STORY

If there is one area that needs strengthening among HBCUs, it is the ability to "tell their story." Too often outsiders, and in fact many who do not have the best interests of HBCUs in mind, are telling the HBCU story. There is much that is good taking place on HBCU campuses, but often the only people who know are those on the actual campus.

When doing the research for this book, we talked with one development officer who spoke of his arrival at his institution. To become acclimated with the campus, he visited each individual college and secured as much literature as possible on its contributions. His goal, being a newcomer, was to gain a better understanding of the college's programs, mission, and communication efforts. One thing that stood out amongst the information was the elaborate newsletters that the majority of the colleges produced. Rivaling many magazines available in the campus bookstore, these 1–3 page circulars illustrated programs that coincided with the University's overall vision and mission. However, upon meeting with the college deans, the development officer learned that the colleges circulated less than 100 copies of these glossy newsletters. The majority of the newsletters were sent to other departments on campus, the board of regents, and a few governmental agencies. While this distribution list is certainly admirable, from a public relations vantage point, it tends to omit the college's alumni—the one constituent group that posseses the natural affinity to the programs and happenings within various schools.

Telling your story to those that benefited the most is a great way of engaging alumni who have not been as involved since graduation, and for those that have stayed connected, this information serves to enhance the value of their degree. Who would not feel better about their college choice after learning of a new accreditation level being achieved or a large research grant being obtained? Knowing that their institution is taking positive strides to enhance the education of tomorrow's leaders makes graduates proud. And, as a benefit to those who have engaged financially; these newsletters telling the institution's story can serve as a donor "thank you."

In addition to having a negative impact on fundraising, not telling the institution's story results in less than accurate (and flattering) depictions by various media outlets. With regard to HBCUs, reporters are curious and ask a lot of questions, such as: Why should Black colleges continue to exist? Why do we need HBCUs in an integrated society or, more frequently now, a "postracial" society? Why are graduation rates so low at some Black colleges? Why is leadership at some HBCUs so heavy handed? And, in recent times, How is the current economic crisis having an impact on HBCUs? Although there are ample individuals who can answer these questions at HBCUs, they are often not doing so, with the exception of a few HBCU leaders. In truth, everyone associated with HBCUs should be able to answer these questions if called upon. Although these kinds of questions are not always fair, being able to provide solid, well thought-out answers is essential–especially when these answers are reported across media outlets of various types. Although these questions are more focused on HBCUs as a whole, it is vital to place an individual HBCU's story within this larger context.

There are quite a few concrete ways to change the conversation about an individual HBCU and HBCUs in general—all in an effort to attract positive national attention from funders. First, HBCU leadership needs to identify experts in the field of higher education who focus on HBCUs in their research and get to know them. These individuals are called by the media, policymakers, and foundations on a regular basis to comment, using empirical data, on HBCUs. It's important to make sure that these people know about your institution and the positive impact it is having on the local community, students, and perhaps, society at larger. The best way to identify these people is to read stories on HBCUs in major newspapers and magazines, including *The New York Times,* the *Wall Street Journal,* the *Washington Post, Diverse: Issues in Higher Education,* the *Chronicle of Higher Education,* the *Chicago Tribune,* and the *Atlanta Journal Constitution,* as these individuals are often cited. We also suggest sending materials on your institution—including annual reports, press releases, campaign materials—to these individuals so that, if appropriate, they can refer to your institution when giving examples to the press. It is also important to send institutional materials to foundations and media outlets. HBCU leaders and fundraisers should keep in mind that funders need to give away their money and the media has to fill pages and airwaves daily.

As mentioned earlier in chapter two, presidents should speak out and write op-eds about their institution's contributions to student success as well as the contributions of HBCUs in general. Op-ed essays should be sent to local, regional, and national papers and magazines. It is best if these op-eds come from the president of an institution, but they can also come from faculty members who are working on noteworthy research projects or student affairs administrators who have discovered ways to retain or graduate more students.

President Barack Obama's presidential campaign demonstrated the profound impact of social media on fundraising and image creation. There is much to be learned from Obama in terms of telling the HBCU story via social networks. All HBCUs need to set up Facebook sites for students, alumni, and supporters to join, creating viral enthusiasm for the institution. Through this media, the institution can keep alumni informed, and more importantly, sing the praises of those faculty and staff who are moving the institution forward. The institution should also highlight the efforts of students and alumni in order to cultivate a personal investment in the institution on behalf of these individuals. In addition, using Facebook allows an HBCU to keep in touch with countless numbers of supporters, announce events, and even garner financial support once they have built up a rapport with users.

Telling the HBCU story also involves sending out more press releases about the accomplishments of the institution. According to research, 70 percent of what is written in newspapers comes directly from press releases. As many HBCUs have limited staffing in the public relations area, having a constant presence in the media can be difficult. However, it is possible and advantageous to engage students in public relations internship opportunities and give them the opportunity to hone their skills. Not only does this give students much needed work experience, but it creates ownership of the institution on the part of the students and this ownership, in turn, may lead to increased engagement as alumni.

We think it is important to acknowledge that the media has had a shaky relationship with HBCUs. Often media stories are negative in tone as most media outlets are looking for ways to attract readers and viewers—a bit of controversy helps when this is your goal. In addition, some Southern newspapers have a long history of antagonizing HBCUs. However, it is possible to couch positive accomplishments of the institution as solutions to longstanding problems of local, regional, or national importance. For example, if the graduation rates are up at an institution, begin the press release with the problem that your institution faced and tell the story of how you are solving it. Media outlets like a comeback story and so do funders.

PUTTING ACADEMICS FIRST

If you take a look at many of the fundraising and admissions brochures for our nation's HBCUs, one thing becomes clear: sports and the marching band are valued. There is nothing wrong with having school spirit and valuing athletic competition. Likewise, HBCUs have boasted amazing marching bands for decades. However, sports and the marching band should be ancillary to academics in truth and image. Although sports are often a window into the college or university experience for potential students, as the NCAA has mentioned in their recent ad campaign, the majority of student athletes "go pro" in something other than sports. All institutions of higher education should emphasize academics first.

Yes, the images of winning football and basketball teams, with all of the glorious colors of the institutions, are engaging, but they should not be the central images in fundraising nor admissions materials. Yes, giving tends to increase after an institution wins a championship—but only for one year. The majority of donors, especially African Americans, give to higher education to support scholarships; donors are not typically motivated by sports images. Giving is stronger when an institution highlights its signature academic programs.

Donors are finicky; they have particular likes and dislikes. If they go to a website and don't see a program that meshes with their interests, they may leave immediately. Likewise, if they go to a website or receive a brochure that has more of a focus on sports than academics, they are sometimes left with an image in their mind—"this institution isn't serious about academics." In reality, HBCUs are serious about academics.

Highlighting sports over academics is a marketing issue and one that has a lasting impact. It tends to reinforce stereotypes about African Americans, implying that they are better at physical activity than intellectual activity. HBCUs need to work hard to dispel the myths around African American intelligence and achievement. Emphasizing the great minds at HBCUs not only empowers future students, it inspires donors, and changes perceptions.

CONNECTING THE HBCU TO NATIONAL ISSUES

One successful strategy for telling an institution's story is to connect to a larger news story. Oftentimes, national reports are released that touch upon the strengths of HBCUs and it is advantageous to connect the institution's strengths and successes to these stories. For example, recently the Urban Institute released a report on HBCUs that have made considerable gains in the STEM areas (science, technology, engineering, and math). The findings in the report were particularly glowing in terms of the environment that HBCUs create in the sciences and their success in terms of sending students to graduate school. Given the increased attention to STEM by federal and state governments, linking the findings of the report to the success and strengths of an individual HBCU could bring positive press to the HBCU.

Another recent opportunity to highlight the success of individual HBCUs came when *The Washington Monthly* released its college rankings. Unlike *US News and World Report*, *The Washington Monthly's* rankings focus on the value added to students and the impact that the institution and its students have on the surrounding community and society as a whole. In these rankings, HBCUs end up at the top due to their historic mission of reaching out to surrounding communities, standing firm on issues of civil rights, and preparing students to be well-rounded citizens. Most of the institutions in the top ten of these rankings were HBCUs. These institutions could benefit from taking the national story and linking the success and efforts of their institutions to it, distributing a more local or regional story to the press.

Yet another way to capitalize on national stories is to look for higher education or societal problems that are in the news. If the HBCU is particularly good at solving these problems or used to face them but has found a way to overcome the problem, a news story that presents the problem but then shows a solution can be shared with local and national media. Media outlets like to present problem-based articles to incite controversy, but they also like a success story and HBCUs can be at the center of that success story. For example, the college graduation rate for African Americans nationally is 43 percent—this fact is of major concern to policymakers, funders, and the higher education community overall. If an HBCU has made significant gains in increasing its graduation rates or has had consistently high graduation rates, there is much that this institution can teach the higher education community. The institution has the potential to attract considerable press and be a leader in terms of African American student success if it tells its story of success to a wide audience.

INSTITUTIONAL BRANDING

Faced with a difficult situation at Paul Quinn College, Michael Sorrell sought to brand the institution and create a positive image that donors, local citizens in the Dallas area, and alumni would embrace. Possibly taking a page from Stephen Colbert's notebook (Colbert Nation), Sorrell began calling the 'Quinnites' Quinnite Nation. He encouraged students to embrace the new idea and communicated it to alumni. In fact, the Paul Quinn website boasts the Quinnite Nation as if it has been a part of the institution for decades. According to Sorrell,

> One of the things we try to do at Paul Quinn is appreciate the effects that the brand has on fundraising and establishing a culture that leaves people feeling good about the institution and the brand of the institution. This is important as we ask for money, favors, or influence. If donors feel good about our brand, they are much more likely to become engaged or give to the institution.

Because of name recognition, it is easier for some HBCUs to brand themselves than others. HBCUs such as Spelman, Morehouse, and Howard have become more well known among funders, those in the larger higher education community, policymakers, and those in the media. However, it is possible to create what Arthur Affleck at Fayetteville State University calls a "buzz" around a lesser known HBCU. According to Affleck,

> People may ask "Who is Fayetteville State?" But it is possible to create a buzz around the institution. You can create some energy and excitement about what you are doing by demonstrating that you have some powerful things happening on your campus.

Affleck offered an example:

> We wrote a proposal years ago for a business man Jamie Diamond entitled "Diamonds in the Rough" and he loved it. We talked about the fact that as an institution we're like a diamond in the rough. We are quality; it's just that you can't see it. Our job is to try to help you see the quality.

Telling the story of the institution is by far one of the most important aspects of fundraising. Without a story, it is nearly impossible to garner funds from anyone but the closest constituents. The president is the chief storyteller of the HBCU but he or she needs the tools to tell a more effective story. Due to the lack of resources at most HBCUs, it is crucial for everyone on the campus to come together to support the storytelling.

Practical Recommendations

- Make sure that all of the good ideas, programs, and aspects of your institution are shared with the outside world. You don't want to be a secret.
- Use positive stories about your individual institution to counter the negative media stories that often surface about HBCUs.
- Share your institutional success with funders and the media on a regular basis.
- Share your institutional success and corresponding data with nationally-known researchers.
- Presidents need to regularly speak out on local and national issues, making a connection to the institution.
- Use social media to promote the success of the institution. Don't underestimate the power of social media and social networks. Those who do are quickly being left behind.
- Make sure to put academics first when telling the story of the institution. Sports and marching band are great side dishes but they aren't the main course at a college.
- Create a "buzz" around the work of the institution or a brand that people recognize as affiliated with the HBCU. Think about what the institution does best and capitalized on it.

9

INNOVATIVE FUNDRAISING AND ENGAGEMENT PROGRAMS

Research suggests that there are not a vast amount of new fundraising programs. Now certainly, with the advent of technology, we are using new methods of connecting such as electronic mail and cellphone texting but the basic premise of aligning donor' interest to institutional needs remains the same. The challenge for HBCUs as well as all charitable organizations is to identify that mixture of fundraising vehicles that meet today's potential supporters where they are and appeals to their specific area of interest. Just like the premise of this book, which recognizes that there are differences associated with fundraising at a Black institution compared to a majority institution, among individual supporters, there are many unique nuances as well. The following examples showcase how many HBCUs are becoming more aware of the need to recognize differences in donors and are creating engagement programs that address a variety of their constituent's interest.

1. ALABAMA A&M UNIVERSITY

Adopt a Band Student Uniform Fundraiser

At a number of HBCUs, the marching band represents a long time moniker for which these institutions are widely known. This was never more evidenced than in the 2002 film *Drumline*, in which the halftime performances rivaled and surpassed the football game, which is supposed to be the main attraction. Recognizing that their own Marching Maroon and White had this type of following, AAMU created a fundraising initiative around its band titled, "Adopt a Band Student Uniform." This effort encourages supporters to underwrite the cost ($500) of one complete band uniform.

2. CLAFLIN UNIVERSITY

FOCUS 100 Student Fund

Established in 2004, the Focus 100 Student Fund assists at-risk students who, through no fault of their own, cannot afford some or all of their books, tuition fees, housing, or are unexpectedly confronted with a financial emergency. This financial bridge allows students to fulfill the dream of graduating from Claflin University.

3. CLARK ATLANTA UNIVERSITY

Alumni Consistent Giving Program

The program asks alumni to make an annual pledge of a minimum of $150. This total amount includes $50.00 for annual Alumni Association dues and the remainder is directed to the University Annual Fund contribution. Annual gifts help maintain a strong alumni support base for the University and are used to jump-start other ongoing fundraising initiatives for the association.

CLASS—Alumni and Schools Campaign

Chapter Leadership and School Support (CLASS) engages graduates and cultivates them for special projects long term. While each year the program format may vary, the university typically hosts one of a four-part alumni reception series designed to touch alumni, encouraging participation and gifts. The remaining three parts are hosted by selected alumni from each of the schools. These are typically done in a reception format where each graduate has an opportunity to speak to peers about the importance of giving.

CUBS—Students Class Gift Campaign

Contributions for the University's Best Students (CUBS) is a student group made up of students from every major and class level, which hosts various events to celebrate student academic success and assists the community at large. Another component of the initiative, The Students Class Gift Campaign encourages each student to make a contribution equal to their class year to the annual fund campaign. This in-school giving experience for students is designed to act as a precursor for establishing a lifelong pattern of giving to the University as well to provide students with greater philanthropic awareness.

PANTHER—Employee Campaign

Payroll Activated Network for Targeted Higher Education Resources (PANTHER) is a faculty and staff annual campaign. Each year employees are sent letters to their on-campus address during the fall, encouraging their participation and giving them the option of designating their gift to the area of their choice including programs, equipment, departments, or the unrestricted fund.

4. DILLARD UNIVERSITY

DU Wants to Know

Asking alumni to fill out surveys and polls engages and empowers them to feel as though their opinion counts. Dillard uses three different types of surveys:

- Alumni Employment and Education Survey (all alumni).
- Alumni Entrepreneurs Survey (alumni business owners, founders, and CEOs).
- Alumni Artists Survey (alumni who are professional visual artists).

5. EDWARD WATERS COLLEGE

Black Male College Explorers Program

Not your typical fundraising or alumni engagement initiative, this intervention program is designed specifically for Black males who are potential high school dropouts and run the risk of never being admitted to college not to mention graduating. Edward Waters College faculty and staff ask middle and high school personnel to identify "at-risk" Black males, grades 7–11. Edward Waters College employees then join forces with the parents and community members to assist these students in developing skills to become independent and self-sufficient adults who will succeed and contribute responsibly in a global community.

6. ELIZABETH CITY STATE UNIVERSITY

GOLD Society

The Graduates of the Last Decade (GOLD) Society strengthen the connection for younger-aged alumni who are up to 10 years out the University and 32 years old or younger. Within the program, there is a development council, which is the leadership for the society, and a networking council. The networking council helps bridge the gap between the young alumni and the University thereby creating a consistent sense of responsibility and lifelong commitment to giving back to Elizabeth City State University.

20/20 Club

The 20/20 Club focuses on increasing the younger generation's knowledge of planned giving and what it means to be philanthropic. Open only to graduates from 1990–1998, the idea is by 2020, these 40–50 year old alumni will have established families and careers and chronologically represent the next generation of major donors.

7. GRAMBLING STATE UNIVERSITY

Legacy Club

The Legacy Club is designed for students whose parent(s), grandparent(s), or great-grandparent(s) are graduates of Grambling State University. The club provides the aforementioned students with various services and activities in an effort to enhance their collegiate experience while at the University. It also creates alumni loyalty, which often results in increased donations.

8. KENTUCKY STATE UNIVERSITY

Thorobred Legacy Project

A number of children, grandchildren, siblings, and others have followed family members and attended Kentucky State University during its 120-year history. The Thorobred Legacy Project, compiles histories of these family members and includes them in video and in print. These stories develop a repository of multigenerational stories of legacy that can be passed on to others. They also create connections between generations of alumni and their children.

9. MORGAN STATE UNIVERSITY

Morgan State University Women

Membership is open to women who are members of the faculty, staff, regents, administration, retirees, wives, student representatives, or from the Morgan community. With a purpose of fostering activities among its members by linking them to opportunities, the organization is poised to generate a great amount of goodwill to the community and more importantly, to the University.

10. NORFOLK STATE UNIVERSITY

Reclamation Program—"The Completion of Your Degree"

The Reclamation Program is designed to facilitate the continuing education and subsequent graduation of Norfolk State University students who have left the institution prior to earning their degree. The project was designed to take full advantage of technology while maintaining academic integrity and the intellectual rigor of Norfolk State University.

11. PAUL QUINN COLLEGE

Be a Fundraiser

Asking alumni and friends to engage and show their support by using social networking technology is a great way to extend the college's fundraising reach. By just clicking the "share link" or "embed form" at the bottom of the donation form, a supporter can post the school's logo and a link to the donation form to their social network—Facebook, Twitter, or LinkedIn.

12. PHILANDER SMITH COLLEGE

"Key Cities" Program

College representatives identified in "Key Cities" throughout the country host special events featuring the president and other executive staff members. This sort of "taking the show on the road" allows the college to meet alumni where they are.

13. PRAIRIE VIEW A&M UNIVERSITY

Panthers at Work

Panthers at Work (PAWS) is a service learning project that allows PVAMU students to learn the value of partnership and civic engagement through community service opportunities. The goal is not just to engage students in community service but to have the students ask and examine larger social questions. Recognized as a community-wide clean-up project, the event is hosted annually and engages University students, faculty, and local citizens in community service projects throughout the county.

14. SAVANNAH STATE UNIVERSITY

SSU Mobile—iPhone App

Savannah State University has its own iPhone application. The app allows for quick and easy access to information on the University wherever you are. Anyone can use the Savannah State suite of apps available for the iPhone to view the latest campus news, sports highlights, classmates, and to navigate your way around campus.

15. SOUTHERN UNIVERSITY AT SHREVEPORT

Jaguary Scholarship Radiothon

The Jaguar Scholarship Radiothon engaged the volunteer services of more than 40 volunteers to staff phone banks, talk to listeners, and solicit pledges. In addition to those on the phones, there is also a fundraising street team that collects additional donations at strategic intersections throughout the city.

16. TRENHOLM STATE TECHNICAL COLLEGE

Seven Course Gala and Auction

The Seven Course Gala and Auction is the primary fundraiser for the college. This special black tie evening event with seven decadent courses features the culinary talents of the students in the Culinary Arts Program led by chefs Maryann Campbell, Robert Cawley, and Rudy Bernard. Proceeds of this event are used to fund Trenholm Tech Foundation initiatives favorable to Trenholm and the planning, design, and construction of a new Culinary Arts facility.

17. UNIVERSITY OF ARKANSAS AT PINE BLUFF

H & R Block Fundraiser

Through a collaboration with H&R Block, UAPB supporters that are new to H&R Block go to a participating location and present the University's referral form. Once confirmed as a new client, H&R Block will donate $25 to the organization.

10

BACKGROUND ON HISTORICALLY BLACK COLLEGES AND UNIVERSITIES

From their arrival on the shores of the United States, African Americans have thirsted for knowledge and viewed education as the key to their freedom. These enslaved people pursued education despite laws, in all Southern states, barring them from learning to read and write. In the North, free Blacks pursued education at three colleges for African Americans: Wilberforce University in Ohio and Lincoln and Cheyney Universities in Pennsylvania. With the end of the Civil War, the enormous task of educating millions of Blacks was shouldered by the federal government, through the Freedman's Bureau, and many Northern church missionaries. As early as 1865, the Freedmen's Bureau began establishing HBCUs, staffed with mainly male staff and teachers with military backgrounds. During the post-Civil War period, most HBCUs were so in name only; these institutions generally provided primary and secondary education during the first decades of their existence.

As noted, religious missionary organizations—some affiliated with Northern White denominations such as the Baptists and Congregationalists and some with Black Churches such as the African Methodist Episcopalians—actively worked with the Freedmen's Bureau. One of the most prominent of the White organizations was the American Missionary Association, but there were many others as well. White northern missionary societies founded HBCUs such as Fisk University in Nashville, Tennessee and Spelman College in Atlanta. The benevolence of these missionaries was tinged with self-interest and often racism. The missionaries' goals in establishing these colleges were to Christianize the freedmen and to rid the country of the "menace" of uneducated Blacks (Anderson, 1988). Among the colleges founded by Black denominations were Morris Brown College in Atlanta, Paul Quinn College in Dallas, and Allen University in Columbia, South Carolina. Distinctive among American colleges, these institutions were founded by Blacks for Blacks (Anderson, 1988). Because these institutions relied on less support from Whites and more support from Black Churches, they were able to plan their own curricula; however, they also were more susceptible to economic downturns and continue to be so in the current day.

With the passage of the second Morrill Act in 1890, the federal government again took an interest in Black education, establishing public Black colleges. This act stipulated that those states practicing segregation in their public colleges and universities would forfeit federal funding unless they established agricultural and mechanical institutions for the Black population (Gasman, 2007). Despite the wording of the Morrill Act, which called for the equitable division of federal funds, these newly-founded institutions received considerably less funding than their White counterparts and thus had inferior facilities and more limited course offerings. Among the 17 new "land-grant" colleges were Prairie View A&M University and Florida A&M University.

By the close of the 19th Century, private Black colleges had used the limited funding received from missionary philanthropists. At roughly the same time, a new kind of philanthropic support materialized—White Northern industrial philanthropy. Among the businessmen who provided this philanthropic support were Andrew Carnegie, James Baldwin, John D. Rockefeller, Julius Rosenwald, and John Foster Peabody. These industry leaders, motivated by a desire to control the various forms of industry, possessed a hint of Christian benevolence (Anderson, 1988). The organization making the most significant contribution to African American higher education was the General Education Board, a collection of White philanthropists created by John D. Rockefeller, Sr., but led by John D. Rockefeller, Jr. Over the first half of the 20th Century, the board gave roughly $63 million to Black higher education, a remarkable figure but only a fraction of what it provided to White colleges and universities (Anderson, 1988). Despite their personal agendas, the funding structure that these industrial giants created was designed in part to control Black education in ways that would benefit the industrial philanthropists by producing graduates skilled in the trades that served the industrialists' enterprises (Anderson, 1988). In particular, the colleges and universities they supported were exceptionally vigilant not to disturb the segregationists' system of racism that ruled the South by the 1890s.

Black institutions such as Hampton and Tuskegee were hallmarks of industrial education. It was at these types of institutions that young African Americans were taught how to shoe horses, sew, cook, and clean under the direction of men such as Samuel Chapman Armstrong at Hampton and his protégé Booker T. Washington at Tuskegee.

Of note, many African American intellectuals opposed the philanthropists' support of industrial education, favoring instead a liberal arts curriculum. Institutions such as Dillard, Howard, Fisk, Spelman, and Morehouse, for example, were more representative of the liberal arts curriculum advocated by W.E.B. Du Bois than of Booker T. Washington's philosophy of advancement through labor and self-sufficiency. Despite the philosophical differences between Washington and Du Bois, the two men both had a goal of educating Blacks and uplifting African Americans as a whole. Basically, Washington favored educating Blacks in the industrial arts so they might become economically self-sufficient, whereas Du Bois wanted to create a Black intellectual elite or "talented tenth" to lead the race toward overall autonomy (Gasman, Baez, & Turner, 2008).

In 1915, the attitudes of the Northern philanthropists changed; they began to shift their attention and funding toward those Black institutions that focused on the liberal arts. Realizing that industrial education could exist alongside a liberal arts curriculum, the philanthropists chose to lend their support more broadly to Black higher education institutions (Anderson, 1988).

The omnipresent power of industrial philanthropy in the early 20th Century led to conservative campuses at Black colleges—campuses that would often tolerate only those presidents and leaders (for the most part White men) who supported or accommodated segregation. Of note, attention from the philanthropists was not especially welcomed by universities such as Fisk, where rebellions broke out against tyrannical leaders whom students labeled puppets of the White philanthropists (Anderson, 1988; Gasman, Baez, & Turner, 2008). Despite these conflicts, industrial philanthropists provided major support for private Black colleges until the late 1930s.

By this time, the White philanthropists had begun to focus their attention elsewhere, providing only scant funding to HBCUs. In response, Frederick D. Patterson, who at the time was president of the Tuskegee Institute, recommended that the country's private Black colleges join forces in their fundraising labors. As a result, in 1944, the leaders of 29 Black colleges and universities came together to create the United Negro College

Fund. The fund began solely as a fundraising organization, but over time it took on advocacy and educational roles as well (Gasman, Baez, & Turner, 2008).

Both public and private Black colleges in the South remained segregated by law and were the only educational option for African Americans until *Brown v. Board of Education* in 1954. Although most institutions of higher education did not experience the same violent fallout from the *Brown* decision as Southern public schools, they were greatly influenced by the decision.

The Supreme Court's ruling meant that HBCUs would be placed in competition with White institutions when recruiting African American students. With the end of legal segregation in *Brown*, many White liberals and some Blacks began to question the future of HBCUs and refer to them as vestiges of segregation. Desegregation proceeded slowly, however, with many public HBCUs and historically White institutions maintaining their racial concentrations even today.

After the *Brown* decision, private HBCUs, which have always been willing to accept students from all backgrounds if the law would allow, struggled to defend issues of quality in an atmosphere that labeled anything all-Black inferior (Gasman, Baez, & Turner, 2008). Many Black colleges also suffered from "brain drain" as predominately White institutions in the North and some in the South made efforts to attract high-achieving Black students once racial diversity became valued in higher education (Gasman, 2007).

The Black college of the 1960s was a much different place from that of the 1920s. The leadership switched from White to Black, and because Blacks had more control over funding, dissent and Black self-determination among the student population were better tolerated (Gasman, 2007). On many public and private Black college campuses throughout the South, students staged sit-ins and protested against segregation and its manifestations throughout the region. Most prominent perhaps were the four students from North Carolina A&T who refused to leave a segregated Woolworth lunch counter in 1960. As Williamson (2008) argues, these student activists were valiant in their fight for civil rights.

During the 1960s the federal government took a greater interest in Black colleges. In an attempt to provide clarity, the Higher Education Act of 1965 defined a Black college as "any ... college or university that was established prior to 1964, whose principal mission was, and is, the education of Black Americans." The recognition of the uniqueness of Black colleges implied in this definition has led to increased federal funding for these institutions.

Another federal intervention on behalf of Black colleges took place in 1980, when President Jimmy Carter signed Executive Order 12232 establishing a national program to alleviate the effects of discriminatory treatment and to strengthen and expand Black colleges to provide quality education. Since then, every U.S. president has renewed the commitment to Black colleges set forth by Carter through this program.

The history of HBCUs continues to shape these institutions in meaningful and positive ways; however, this history also confines HBCUs from time to time. Often when outsiders are familiar only with the history of HBCUs, they fail to see what is currently happening, including these institutions' service to diverse constituencies, their enormous track record in the sciences, and their continuing and crucial role in educating those African Americans who eventually occupy the Black middle class.

11

CONCLUDING THOUGHTS

There are many standard practices in fundraising. However, fundraising within the HBCU context is unique and requires the participation of the entire campus. Successful fundraising requires an 'all campus approach' with the assistance of upper level administrators, faculty, student services staff, students, and alumni. Each of these groups needs to understand the role that they play and the impact that they have on the financial stability of the HBCU. As we have demonstrated throughout this book, HBCUs are an important part of the higher education landscape and are deserving of support from both internal and external constituencies. They are contributing in meaningful ways to their surrounding communities as well as on a national level. Having a systematic approach to fundraising is essential to the future of HBCUs.

The fact is that we know what works both in overall fundraising and within the HBCU context. We have superb models of success and many stellar leaders within the HBCU community, but we need to learn from these examples and emulate their success. It is time to make improvements and changes in fundraising at HBCUs across the board. The very survival of these institutions depends on it.

After cleaning house and doing a full assessment of the fundraising strengths and weaknesses of the institution, those in institutional advancement along with the HBCU president, need to review the institution's strategic plan. The fundraising strategy should be directly tied to the strategic plan; in fact, the plan should drive the fundraising strategy.

HBCU leaders and their advancement staffs need to remember the value of the small and average donor. These individuals are the life-blood of the institution. They contribute to the annual fund as well as other initiatives. They are often slow and steady, lending consistency to the fundraising process and increasing the alumni giving percentage. Young alumni are also increasingly important. The United States is experiencing one of the biggest participation rates in service learning in our history and HBCUs can capitalize on this. Young people are eager to get involved and this type of involvement leads to organizational commitment, which eventually leads to monetary contributions.

Those leaders in the institutional advancement area must take advantage of all available opportunities for professional development. Although there are fundraising trainings or sessions at national conferences, only a fraction of HBCU leaders and staff attend—even when the registration and travel fees are complimentary. HBCUs cannot afford to miss opportunities for professional development that enhance fundraising skills. These sessions need to be attended by not only those in fundraising, but also presidents, deans, and those in student affairs.

HBCU leaders, especially presidents, must be more visible. They must contribute to national dialogues, speaking out on national issues and those issues of concern in their local communities. Not only does speaking out and being brave command the respect of alumni, it also attracts the attention of funders and those in the media. Attention from all of these entities can lead to more resources. In addition to fundraisers and academic leaders, presidents also need to be thought leaders.

Presidents need to think strategically about the membership of the institution's board of trustees. These individuals must make a full commitment to the success, financial stability, and sustainability of the HBCU. They also need to agree to either give money at the lead gift level or secure funding from other individuals. Board members who fail to contribute to the institution are a liability as they take up precious space that could be filled by an individual with a willingness to give.

Those in institutional advancement, with the support of the president, must convey the importance of the role that is played by faculty members and students services staff. These two entities have the closest relationship with students while they are on campus. Faculty members should be encouraged to stay in touch with students and share information on student successes and whereabouts. Student services staff members must be held to a high standard—one in which mediocrity is not tolerated. For too long, according to both evidence and anecdote, many of those in student services have not lived up to the potential of the HBCU community. There are times when an outside force is needed to upset the status quo and to make much needed change.

Leaders in institutional advancement also need to spend time educating alumni on their central role in the college or university. These individuals are one of the greatest resources of the institution if cultivated early, respectfully, and properly. Often alumni need to know how to be involved in their alma mater and it is the role of the advancement staff to provide them with options.

HBCUs need to capitalize on the communal nature of Black culture and the predisposition toward group membership (a holdover from safe spaces during segregation). African Americans are more likely to give philanthropically if asked by someone they know and trust. As such, working with affinity groups that cater to the needs of Blacks can be advantageous. Remembering where alumni had allegiances as students is essential to understanding what will motivate them to become involved as adults.

Lastly, HBCUs must change their approach to working with funders. For too long, HBCUs have placed an emphasis on needs rather than successes. Although all HBCUs, and colleges and universities for that matter, have needs, we are living in an educational culture of success and messages of success and accomplishment resonate with funders. In order to secure funding, the HBCU must show where it has been successful.

AND THE FUTURE HOLDS ...

Just as colleges and universities overall are rapidly changing, so are HBCUs. It is vital that they keep up with these changes and move forward in order to sustain the future of these important institutions. Below, we offer several future-focused recommendations for HBCUs. These recommendations are aimed at increasing fundraising success, but they will also enhance the entire campus including its reputation, efficiency, and performance.

First, HBCUs need to grow their own fundraisers. Fundraising within the HBCU environment requires special skills and a love of the institution. HBCUs themselves are the perfect place to create a fundraising training program that draws upon more general fundraising skills, but also focuses on the unique strengths and challenges that take place within the HBCU environment. We hope that one or more HBCUs will take the lead and create a fundraising program. This is essential to the future strength of HBCUs.

Second, HBCUs are becoming more and more diverse with growing numbers of White, Latino, and Asian students. Given the changing demographics of the country, in the very near future, many HBCUs will also be Hispanic Serving Institutions. Some HBCUs are reframing their strategic plans to embrace this increased diversity. However, HBCUs also need to be prepared to reframe their fundraising strategy. There is ample research that shows that the various racial and ethnic groups respond to different types of cultivation strategies and HBCUs need to become more familiar with these strategies (Gow-Pettey, 2001; Neuwman, 2002; Smith et al., 1999). This can be done by reading those books available on the topic, by hosting focus groups with non-Black students and alumni, and by attending conference sessions focused on philanthropy in communities of color.

Third, although websites have been around for 20 years now, HBCUs need to move their web presence to a new level. A first response to this suggestion might be, "we don't have the resources," but the truth is that HBCUs have immense human resources in the form of tech savvy students who know how to create their own presence on the web and could be assisting their HBCU. Institutions would benefit from having students critique websites for awkward transitions, missing information, and stylistic issues. Alumni with technological expertise could also be brought in to assist with enhancing the HBCU's web presence. First and foremost, HBCUs must make it easier for donors to give to their institution. It's a shame and a loss of funds when a donor visits the website and can't find the "GIVE" button. This button ought to be one of the first things a website viewer sees—this along with some major successes and a link to the admissions part of the site. Demonstrating success, increasing enrollment, and providing opportunities to give should be the central focus of the HBCU website.

Fourth, although we talked about social media and its importance earlier in the book, we want to emphasize the need for HBCU presidents to have a voice and presence on various forms of social media. According to the Pew Research Center's Project on Excellence in Journalism (www.journalism.org), Facebook is the number two driver of consumers to news websites after Google. Facebook has created a culture of sharing news, cultural happenings, and opportunities (including educational opportunities) and people of all ages are using it. Presidents of HBCUs need to participate in these forms of social media either independently or through the public relations office. Those presidents who are active already, including Walter Kimbrough of Philander Smith, Michael Sorrell at Paul Quinn, Julianne Malveaux of Bennett College for Women, and Robert Franklin at Morehouse, are ahead of the game. They not only share information about their own institution but they share news stories that relate to HBCUs, African Americans, education, and the nation overall. They each have a healthy following and have enhanced the reputation of their institutions. Their presence even acts as a draw in terms of enrollment as potential students like to see a "cool" president who keeps up with trends.

Lastly, we urge readers to push themselves and to think in the most innovative ways about improving their HBCU. Settling for the status quo gives critics the ammunition that they need to tear down HBCUs and to chip away at their successes. Being on the cutting edge and trying new things in the area of fundraising is essential for HBCUs. But, more than that—innovative strategies need to be discussed. HBCU leaders in institutional advancement need to present their ideas at conferences, write about them in national publications, and share them with other HBCUs. Talking about how you became successful is just as important as talking about that success.

FEDERAL GRANTS AVAILABLE TO HBCUs

Name of Grant Opportunity	Sponsor
ADVANCE: Increasing the Participation and Advancement of Women in Academic Science and Engineering Careers	National Science Foundation
Alliances for Broadening Participation in STEM (ABP)	National Science Foundation
Broadening Participation in Computing (BPC)	National Science Foundation
Broadening participation Research Initiation Grants in Engineering (BRIGE)	National Science Foundation
Centers of Research Excellence in Science and Technology (CREST) and HBCU Research Infrastructure for Science and Engineering (RISE)	National Science Foundation
Cyberinfrastructure Training, Education, Advancement, and Mentoring for our 21st Century Workforce (CI-TEAM)	National Science Foundation

Name of Grant Opportunity	Sponsor
George E. Brown, Jr. Network for Earthquake Engineering Simulation Research (NEESR)	National Science Foundation
Geoscience Education	National Science Foundation
Historically Black Colleges and Universities Undergraduate Program (HBCU-UP)	National Science Foundation
Innovative Technology Experiences for Students and Teachers (ITEST)	National Science Foundation
Integrative Graduate Education and Research Traineeship (IGERT) Program	National Science Foundation
Partnerships in Astronomy & Astrophysics Research and Education (PAARE) Undergraduate Research and Mentoring	National Science Foundation
(URM) in the Biological Sciences	National Science Foundation
Academic Career Award (Parent K07)	National Institutes of Health
Academic Research Enhancement Award	National Institutes of Health
Blueprint Program for Enhancing Neuroscience Diversity through Undergraduate Research Education Experiences (R25)	National Institutes of Health
Community Participation in Research (R01) Community Participation Research Targeting the Medically Underserved (R01)	National Institutes of Health National Institutes of Health
Cutting-Edge Basic Research Awards (CEBRA)	National Institutes of Health
Health Promotion Among Racial and Ethnic Minority Males (R21)	National Institutes of Health
Health Research with Diverse Populations (R01)	National Institutes of Health

Name of Grant Opportunity	*Sponsor*
Institutional Clinical and Translational Science Award	National Institutes of Health
Minority Access to Research Careers (MARC) Ancillary Training Activities	National Institutes of Health
NIAID Science Education Awards (R25)	National Institutes of Health
NIDCD Small Grant Program (R03)	National Institutes of Health
NIH Small Research Grant Program (Parent R03)	National Institutes of Health
Partnerships for Biodefense (R01)	National Institutes of Health
Reducing Health Disparities Among Minority and Underserved Children (R21)	National Institutes of Health
Research Project Grant (Parent R01)	National Institutes of Health
Research Supplements to Promote Diversity in Health-Related Research	National Institutes of Health
Ruth L. Kirschstein National Research Service Award (NRSA) Institutional Research Training Grants (T32)	National Institutes of Health
Seeding National Mentoring Networks to Enhance Diversity of the Mental Health Research Workforce (U24)	National Institutes of Health
The Effect of Racial and Ethnic Discrimination/Bias on Health Care Delivery	National Institutes of Health
Broadband Technology Opportunities Program and Rural Utilities Service Broadband Initiative Program	Department of Commerce
DHS HS-STEM Career Development Grants	Department of Homeland Security

Name of Grant Opportunity	Sponsor
Historically Black College and University Capital Financing Program (Loan)	Department of Education
Historically Black Colleges and Universities Program	Department of Education
Minority Science and Engineering Improvement Program	Department of Education
Historic Preservation Fund-National Park Service	U.S. Department of Interior
Minority Serving Institutions Program (MSIP)	U.S. Nuclear Regulatory Program
Awards for Faculty at Historically Black Colleges and Universities	National Endowment for the Humanities
Faculty Research Awards	National Endowment for the Humanities
Diversity Initiative	Andrew Mellon Foundation
Historically Black Colleges & Universities	Andrew Mellon Foundation
Innovation Generation Collaborative Grant	Motorola Foundation
Innovation Generation Grant	Motorola Foundation
Innovation Generation University Grant	Motorola Foundation
Minority Serving Institutions Leadership Fellows Models of Success	National Forum for Higher Education for the Public Good Lumina Foundation for Education
Microsoft Dynamics Academic Alliance	Microsoft Corporation
Innovations in Education	Hewlett Packard Foundation
Committee for Research and Exploration	National Geographic

INTERVIEW QUESTIONS

1. Describe your role in your institution's fundraising approach:

   a. Did you come to your position with any fundraising experience?
   b. On average, how much of your week is allocated to fundraising?
   c. Are you accessible for donor visits and interactions?
   d. Do you see your involvement increasing?

2. Describe a recent solicitation you were involved in:

   a. Who set it up?
   b. What was the target ask?
   c. Who made the ask?

3. Fundraising team:

   a. How is it structured?
   b. How often do you and the fundraising team meet?
   c. Do you meet with the team or only the vice president?

4. In addition to Institutional Advancement:

   a. Is there a requirement for others to get involved in fundraising on your campus?
   b. Are staff outside the realm of fundraising given educational opportunities to understand their role in achieving the institution's development goals? (e.g. Financial aid counselors learning to be more customer-based focused to ensure that students leave with positive memories, and thus have a stronger proclivity to donate.)
   c. Is the academic side of the institution involved in fundraising? Why/ Why not?
   d. What department should be on the fundraising team that is not currently?
   e. What accountability measures are in place for the fundraising team?

5. Institutional fundraising goals:

   a. How were they determined?
   b. How are they measured?
   c. How often are the goals re-evaluated?

6. For Private College presidents or Publics with a Foundation Board:

   a. What role does your board of trustees play in fundraising?
   b. What is the minimum gift expected of board of trustee members?
   c. How much money are board members expected to raise?

HISTORICALLY BLACK COLLEGES AND UNIVERSITIES, GENERAL CHARACTERISTICS

Institution	Year of Est.	Address	Type	Tuition & Fees (2009–10)
Alabama A&M University	1875	4900 Meridian Street, Normal, Alabama 35762	4-year, Public	$4,692
Alabama State University	1875	915 S. Jackson Street, Montgomery, Alabama 36101–0271	4-year, Public	$6,468
Albany State University	1903	504 College Drive, Albany, Georgia 31705	4-year, Public	$4,060
Alcorn State University	1871	1000 ASU Drive Ste 359, Alcorn State, Mississippi 39096–7500	4-year, Public	$4,498
Allen University	1870	1530 Harden Street, Columbia, South Carolina 29204	4-year, Private	$11,285
Arkansas Baptist College	1884	1621 Dr. Martin Luther King Drive, Little Rock, Arkansas 72202–6099	4-year, Private	$7,018
Barber-Scotia College	1867	145 Cambarrus Avenue West, Concord, North Carolina 28025–5143	4-year, Private	N/A
Benedict College	1870	1600 Harden Street, Columbia, South Carolina 29204–1086	4-year, Private	$15,590
Bennett College for Women	1873	900 E. Washington Street, Greensboro, North Carolina 27401–3239	4-year, Private	$15,234
Bethune-Cookman University	1904	640 Dr. Mary McLeod Bethune Blvd, Daytona Beach, Florida 32114–3099	2-year, Public	$12,936
Bishop State Community College	1927	351 North Broad Street, Mobile, Alabama 36603–5898	2-year, Public	$2,700
Bluefield State College	1895	219 Rock Street, Bluefield, West Virginia 24701	4-year, Public	$4,596

Institution	Year of Est.	Address	Type	Tuition & Fees (2009–10)
Bowie State University	1865	14000 Jericho Park Road, Bowie, Maryland 20715–9465	4-year, Public	$6,039
Central State University	1887	1400 Brush Row Road, Wilberforce, Ohio 45384–1004	4-year, Public	$5,294
Cheyney University of Pennsylvania	1837	1837 University Circle, Cheyney, Pennsylvania 19319–0200	4-year, Public	$7,360
Claflin University	1869	400 Magnolia Street, Orangeburg, South Carolina 29115–4498	4-year, Private	$12,666
Clark Atlanta University	1988	223 James P Brawley Drive, S.W., Atlanta, Georgia 30314–4391	4-year, Private	$17,038
Clinton Junior College	1894	1029 Crawford Road, Rock Hill, South Carolina 29730	2-year, Private	$3,635
Coahoma Community College	1924	3240 Friars Point Road, Clarksdale, Mississippi 38614	2-year, Private	$1,840
Concordia College-Selma	1922	1804 Green Street, Selma, Alabama 36701	4-year, Private	$7,370
Coppin State University	1900	2500 West North Avenue, Baltimore, Maryland 21216–3698	4-year, Public	$5,441
Delaware State University	1891	1200 N. Dupont Highway, Dover, Delaware 19901	4-year, Public	$6,481
Denmark Technical College	1947	1126 Solomon Blatt Blvd, Denmark, South Carolina 29042	2-year, Public	$2,398

Institution	Founded	Address	Type	Tuition
Dillard University	1896	2601 Gentilly Blvd, New Orleans, Louisiana 70122	4-year, Private	$13,880
Edward Waters College	1866	1658 Kings Road, Jacksonville, Florida 32209	4-year, Private	$9,990
Elizabeth City State University	1891	1704 Weeksville Road, Elizabeth City, North Carolina 27909	4-year, Public	$3,031
Fayetteville State University	1867	1200 Murchison Road, Fayetteville, North Carolina 28301–4298	4-year, Public	$3,177
Fisk University	1866	1000 17th Avenue North, Nashville, Tennessee 37208–4501	4-year, Private	$17,060
Florida A&M University	1887	Tallahassee, Florida 32307	4-year, Public	$3,958
Florida Memorial University	1879	15800 NW 42 Avenue, Miami Gardens, Florida 33054–6199	4-year, Private	$13,356
Fort Valley State University	1895	1005 State University Drive, Fort Valley, Georgia 31030–4313	4-year, Public	$5,012
Gadsden State Community College	1925	1001 George Wallace Drive, Gadsden, Alabama 35903	2-year, Public	$2,700
Grambling State University	1901	403 Main Street, Grambling, Louisiana 71245	4-year, Public	$4,016
Hampton University	1868	Hampton, Virginia 23668–0099	4-year, Private	$17,212
Harris-Stowe State University	1857	34175 Highway 18, Utica, Missouri 39175	4-year, Public	$4,336
Hinds Community College-Utica	1917	3026 Laclede Avenue, Saint Louis, Missouri 63103–2136	2-year, Public	N/A

Institution	Year of Est.	Address	Type	Tuition & Fees (2009–10)
Howard University	1867	2400 Sixth Street N.W., Washington, District of Columbia 20059–0001	4-year, Private	$16,075
Huston-Tillotson University	1881	900 Chicon Street, Austin, Texas 78702–2795	4-year, Private	$11,434
Interdenominational Theological Center	1958	700 Martin Luther King Jr Drive, Atlanta, Georgia 30314–4143	4-year, Private	N/A
Jackson State University	1877	1440 J R Lynch Street, Jackson, Mississippi 39217	4-year, Public	$4,634
J.F. Drake State Technical College	1961	3421 Meridian Street N., Huntsville, Alabama 35811	2-year, Public	$2,700
Jarvis Christian College	1912	Hwy 80 E, Hawkins, Texas 75765–1470	4-year, Private	$9,608
Johnson C. Smith University	1867	100 Beatties Ford Road, Charlotte, North Carolina 28216–5398	4-year, Private	$15,754
Kentucky State University	1886	400 East Main Street, Frankfort, Kentucky 40601–2355	4-year, Public	$5,686
Knoxville College	1875	901 Knoxville College Drive, Knoxville, TN 37921	4-year, Private	N/A
Lane College	1862	545 Lane Avenue, Jackson, Tennessee 38301–4598	4-year, Private	$8,000
Langston University	1897	102 Page Hall, Langston, Oklahoma 73050	4-year, Public	$3,827

Institution	Founded	Address	Type	Tuition
Lawson State Community College-Birmingham Campus	N/A	3060 Wilson Road S.W., Birmingham, Alabama 35221–1717	2-year, Public	$3,000
Le Moyne-Owen College	1871	807 Walker Avenue, Memphis, Tennessee 38126–6595	4-year, Private	$10,298
Lewis College of Business	1928	LCB Online, 17370 Meyers Road, Detroit, Michigan 48235	2-year, Private	N/A
Lincoln University	1866	820 Chestnut Street, Jefferson City, Missouri 65101	4-year, Public	$4,948
Lincoln University of Pennsylvania	1854	1570 Baltimore Pike, Lincoln University, Pennsylvania 19352–0999	4-year, Public	$8,222
Livingstone College	1879	701 W Monroe Street, Salisbury, North Carolina 28144	4-year, Private	$13,658
Meharry Medical College	1876	1005 DB Todd Blvd, Nashville, Tennessee 37208	4-year, Private	N/A
Miles College	1898	5500 Myron Massey Blvd, Fairfield, Alabama 35064–2621	4-year, Private	$9,164
Mississippi Valley State University	1950	14000 Highway 82 West, Itta Bena, Mississippi 38941–1400	4-year, Public	$4,877
Morehouse College	1867	830 Westview Drive S.W., Atlanta, Georgia 30314	4-year, Private	$21,376
Morehouse School of Medicine	1875	720 Westview Drive S.W., Atlanta, Georgia 30310–1495	4-year, Private	N/A
Morgan State University	1867	1700 East Cold Spring Lane, Baltimore, Maryland 21251–0001	4-year, Public	$6,548

Institution	Year of Est.	Address	Type	Tuition & Fees (2009–10)
Morris Brown College	1881	643 Martin Luther King Jr. Drive, Atlanta, Georgia 30314	4-year, Private	N/A
Morris College	1908	100 West College Street, Sumter, South Carolina 29150–3599	4-year, Private	$9,901
Norfolk State University	1935	700 Park Avenue, Norfolk, Virginia 23504–8000	4-year, Public	$5,872
North Carolina A&T State University	1891	1601 E Market Street, Greensboro, North Carolina 27411	4-year, Public	$3,696
North Carolina Central University	1910	1801 Fayetteville Street, Durham, North Carolina 27707	4-year, Public	$3,922
Oakwood University	1896	7000 Adventist Blvd NW, Huntsville, Alabama 35896	4-year, Private	$13,834
Paine College	1882	1235 15th Street, Augusta, Georgia 30901–3182	4-year, Private	$11,794
Paul Quinn College	1872	3837 Simpson Stuart Road, Dallas, Texas 75241	4-year, Private	$10,650
Philander Smith College	1877	900 W. Daisy Bates Drive, Little Rock, Arkansas 72202–3799	4-year, Private	$9,000
Prairie View A&M University	1876	FM 1098 Road & University Drive, Prairie View, Texas 77446	4-year, Public	$6,763
Rust College	1866	150 Rust Avenue, Holly Springs, Mississippi 38635	4-year, Private	$7,870

Institution	Founded	Location	Type	Tuition
Saint Augustine's College	1867	1315 Oakwood Avenue, Raleigh, North Carolina 27610–2298	4-year, Private	$15,690
Saint Paul's College	1888	115 College Drive, Lawrenceville, Virginia 23868	4-year, Private	$13,210
Saint Philip's College	1898	1801 Martin Luther King Drive, San Antonio, Texas 78203–2098	2-year, Public	$1,562
Savannah State University	1890	3219 College Street, Savannah, Georgia 31404–5310	4-year, Public	$4,774
Selma University	1878	1501 Lapsley Street, Dinkins Hall, Selma, Alabama 36701	4-year, Private	$3,760
Shaw University	1865	118 East South Street, Raleigh, North Carolina 27601	2-year, Private	$11,696
Shelton State Community College	1952	9500 Old Greensboro Road, Tuscaloosa, Alabama 35405–8522	2-year, Public	$2,700
Shorter College	1886	604 Locust Street, North Little Rock, Arkansas 72114	2-year, Private	N/A
South Carolina State University	1896	300 College Street N.E., Orangeburg, South Carolina 29117–0001	4-year, Public	$8,462
Southern University and A&M College	1880	Southern Branch Post Office, Baton Rouge, Louisiana 70813	4-year, Public	$4,100
Southern University at New Orleans	1956	6400 Press Drive, New Orleans, Louisiana 70126	4-year, Public	$3,072
Southern University at Shreveport	1967	3050 Martin Luther King Drive, Shreveport, Louisiana 71107	4-year, Public	$2,464

Institution	Year of Est.	Address	Type	Tuition & Fees (2009–10)
Southwestern Christian College	1948	200 Bowser Circle, Terrell, Texas 75160–4812	4-year, Private	$6,185
Spelman College	1881	350 Spelman Lane SW, Atlanta, Georgia 30314–4399	4-year, Private	$20,926
Stillman College	1876	3601 Stillman Blvd, Tuscaloosa, Alabama 35403	4-year, Private	$13,462
Talladega College	1867	627 W Battle Street, Talladega, Alabama 35160	4-year, Private	$8,940
Tennessee State University	1912	3500 John Merritt Blvd, Nashville, Tennessee 37209–1561	4-year, Public	$5,414
Texas College	1894	2404 N. Grand Avenue, Tyler, Texas 75702	4-year, Private	$9,490
Texas Southern University	1927	3100 Cleburne Street, Houston, Texas 77004	4-year, Public	$6,401
Tougaloo College	1869	500 W County Line Road, Tougaloo, Mississippi 39174	4-year, Private	$9,718
Trenholm State Technical College	2001	1225 Air Base Blvd, Montgomery, Alabama 36108–3199	2-year, Public	$2,700
Tuskegee University	1861	Kresge Center, 3rd Floor, Tuskegee, Alabama 36088–1920	4-year, Private	$16,280
University of Arkansas at Pine Bluff	1873	1200 N University Mail Slot 4789, Pine Bluff, Arkansas 71601	4-year, Public	$4,796
University of Maryland Eastern Shore	1886	J.T. Williams Hall, Princess Anne, Maryland 21853–1299	4-year, Public	$6,082

Institution	Year	Address	Type	Tuition
University of the District of Columbia	1851	4200 Connecticut Avenue N.W., Washington, District of Columbia 20008	4-year, Public	$3,000
University of the Virgin Islands	1962	2 John Brewers Bay, Charlotte Amalie, Virgin Islands 00802–9990	4-year, Public	$4,150
Virginia State University	1882	One Hayden Drive, Petersburg, Virginia 23806	4-year, Private	$6,174
Virginia Union University	1865	1500 N Lombardy Street, Richmond, Virginia 23220	4-year, Private	$13,934
Virginia University of Lynchburg	1886	2058 Garfield Avenue, Lynchburg, Virginia 24501	4-year, Private	$4,300
Voorhees College	1897	481 Porter Drive, Denmark, South Carolina 29042	4-year, Private	$10,164
West Virginia State University	1891	Rte 25, Institute, West Virginia 25112–1000	4-year, Public	$4,524
Wilberforce University	1865	1055 N Bickett Road, Wilberforce, Ohio 45384–1001	4-year, Private	$12,470
Wiley College	1873	711 Wiley Avenue, Marshall, Texas 75670	4-year, Private	$9,970
Winston-Salem State University	1892	601 Martin Luther King Jr Drive, Winston-Salem, North Carolina 27110–0001	4-year, Public	$3,522
Xavier University of Louisiana	1915	One Drexel Drive, New Orleans, Louisiana 70125–1098	4-year, Private	$16,300

Sources: United States Department of Education (2011). Data on Historically Black Colleges and Universities. Retrieved from http://nces.ed.gov/ipeds/datacenter

United States Department of Education (2011). List of Historically Black Colleges and Universities. Retrieved from http://www2.ed.gov/about/inits/list/whhbcu/edlite-list.html

HISTORICALLY BLACK COLLEGES AND UNIVERSITIES, ENROLLMENT, RETENTION, AND GRADUATION

Institution	Total Enrollment (2009–10)	6-Year Graduation Rate (2009)	Full-time Retention Rate (2009)	Part-time Retention Rate (2009)
Alabama A&M University	5,327	29%	69%	50%
Alabama State University	5,564	22%	53%	27%
Albany State University	4,473	42%	77%	67%
Alcorn State University	3,334	38%	70%	20%
Allen University	827	19%	62%	N/A
Arkansas Baptist College	640	3%	64%	63%
Barber-Scotia College	N/A	N/A	N/A	N/A
Benedict College	2,983	31%	60%	27%
Bennett College for Women	766	48%	76%	33%
Bethune-Cookman University	3,637	36%	71%	100%
Bishop State Community College	3,598	N/A	50%	36%
Bluefield State College	1,989	24%	61%	100%
Bowie State University	5,617	39%	70%	43%
Central State University	2,436	19%	57%	38%
Cheyney University of Pennsylvania	1,488	24%	60%	10%
Claflin University	1,860	47%	72%	N/A
Clark Atlanta University	3,873	43%	65%	11%
Clinton Junior College	148	N/A	88%	N/A
Coahoma Community College	2,565	N/A	51%	29%

Institution	Total Enrollment (2009–10)	6-Year Graduation Rate (2009)	Full-time Retention Rate (2009)	Part-time Retention Rate (2009)
Concordia College-Selma	568	17%	38%	7%
Coppin State University	3,801	14%	62%	53%
Delaware State University	3,609	34%	66%	33%
Denmark Technical College	1,105	N/A	34%	4%
Dillard University	1,011	28%	70%	N/A
Edward Waters College	831	12%	51%	0%
Elizabeth City State University	3,264	46%	76%	50%
Fayetteville State University	6,283	32%	74%	0%
Fisk University	650	57%	81%	0%
Florida A&M University	12,274	39%	78%	50%
Florida Memorial University	1,923	37%	68%	75%
Fort Valley State University	3,553	31%	71%	38%
Gadsden State Community College	6,917	N/A	55%	46%
Grambling State University	4,992	29%	56%	10%
Hampton University	5,402	52%	77%	52%
Harris-Stowe State University	1,886	21%	45%	9%
Hinds Community College-Utica	1,917	N/A	N/A	N/A
Howard University	10,573	62%	83%	57%
Huston-Tillotson University	882	29%	55%	N/A

Institution				
Interdenominational Theological Center	421	N/A	N/A	N/A
Jackson State University	8,783	47%	76%	64%
Jarvis Christian College	628	11%	41%	N/A
J.F. Drake State Technical College	1,258	N/A	47%	30%
Johnson C. Smith University	1,466	38%	69%	N/A
Kentucky State University	2,834	23%	52%	6%
Knoxville College	100	N/A	N/A	N/A
Lane College	2,146	25%	61%	100%
Langston University	2,749	27%	57%	N/A
Lawson State Community College-Birmingham Campus	4,353	N/A	54%	55%
Le Moyne-Owen College	890	16%	64%	7%
Lewis College of Business	300	N/A	N/A	N/A
Lincoln University	3,314	25%	52%	28%
Lincoln University of Pennsylvania	2,649	37%	74%	50%
Livingstone College	1,082	28%	51%	25%
Meharry Medical College	786	N/A	N/A	N/A
Miles College	1,791	21%	74%	16%
Mississippi Valley State University	2,850	35%	61%	100%
Morehouse College	2,689	60%	81%	25%
Morehouse School of Medicine	326	N/A	N/A	N/A
Morgan State University	7,226	32%	68%	50%

Institution	Total Enrollment (2009–10)	6-Year Graduation Rate (2009)	Full-time Retention Rate (2009)	Part-time Retention Rate (2009)
Morris Brown College	240	N/A	N/A	N/A
Morris College	966	30%	56%	100%
Norfolk State University	6,993	32%	70%	37%
North Carolina A&T State University	10,614	37%	77%	33%
North Carolina Central University	8,587	44%	77%	56%
Oakwood University	1,916	40%	72%	50%
Paine College	907	28%	58%	N/A
Paul Quinn College	171	12%	9%	N/A
Philander Smith College	668	21%	72%	25%
Prairie View A & M University	8,608	32%	71%	40%
Rust College	1,072	18%	48%	37%
Saint Augustine's College	1,529	48%	62%	8%
Saint Paul's College	584	17%	40%	100%
Saint Philip's College	11,008	N/A	51%	38%
Savannah State University	3,820	29%	72%	38%
Selma University	35	N/A	100%	100%
Shaw University	2,538	34%	52%	46%
Shelton State Community College	5,808	N/A	58%	58%
Shorter College	N/A	N/A	N/A	N/A

South Carolina State University	4,538	36%	67%	26%
Southern University and A&M College	7,619	30%	72%	80%
Southern University at New Orleans	3,141	8%	47%	43%
Southern University at Shreveport	3,014	N/A	54%	58%
Southwestern Christian College	201	N/A	66%	N/A
Spelman College	2,229	83%	84%	30%
Stillman College	1,041	21%	55%	63%
Talladega College	700	22%	54%	15%
Tennessee State University	8,824	40%	67%	45%
Texas College	964	8%	51%	20%
Texas Southern University	9,394	11%	67%	61%
Tougaloo College	939	42%	74%	N/A
Trenholm State Technical College	1,733	N/A	63%	45%
Tuskegee University	2,931	41%	65%	N/A
University of Arkansas at Pine Bluff	3,792	25%	64%	19%
University of Maryland Eastern Shore	4,433	32%	70%	45%
University of the District of Columbia	4,960	12%	57%	41%
University of the Virgin Islands	2,602	25%	75%	56%
Virginia State University	5,366	44%	67%	63%
Virginia Union University	1,691	35%	51%	0%
Virginia University of Lynchburg	327	N/A	100%	96%
Voorhees College	701	25%	63%	N/A

Institution	Total Enrollment (2009–10)	6-Year Graduation Rate (2009)	Full-time Retention Rate (2009)	Part-time Retention Rate (2009)
West Virginia State University	4,003	24%	60%	50%
Wilberforce University	710	30%	61%	100%
Wiley College	1,237	23%	62%	40%
Winston-Salem State University	6,427	36%	78%	50%
Xavier University of Louisiana	3,338	45%	69%	60%

Source: United States Department of Education (2011). Data on Historically Black Colleges and Universities. Retrieved from http://nces.ed.gov/ipeds/datacenter

APPENDIX E

HISTORICALLY BLACK COLLEGES AND UNIVERSITIES, FINANCIAL AID

Institute	Total Enrollment (2009–10)	% of Full-time First-time Undergraduates Receiving Financial Aid (2008–09)	% of Full-time First-time Undergraduates Receiving Pell Grants (2008–09)
Alabama A&M University	5,327	92%	49%
Alabama State University	5,564	96%	73%
Albany State University	4,473	97%	69%
Alcorn State University	3,334	70%	70%
Allen University	827	83%	78%
Arkansas Baptist College	640	47%	40%
Barber-Scotia College	N/A	N/A	N/A
Benedict College	2,983	99%	80%
Bennett College for Women	766	97%	64%
Bethune-Cookman University	3,637	98%	70%
Bishop State Community College	3,598	83%	73%

Institute	Total Enrollment (2009–10)	% of Full-time First-time Undergraduates Receiving Financial Aid (2008–09)	% of Full-time First-time Undergraduates Receiving Pell Grants (2008–09)
Bluefield State College	1,989	90%	56%
Bowie State University	5,617	89%	46%
Central State University	2,436	97%	75%
Cheyney University of Pennsylvania	1,488	97%	66%
Claflin University	1,860	95%	71%
Clark Atlanta University	3,873	89%	57%
Clinton Junior College	148	100%	100%
Coahoma Community College	2,565	96%	92%
Concordia College-Selma	568	100%	100%
Coppin State University	3,801	84%	60%
Delaware State University	3,609	94%	50%
Denmark Technical College	1,105	97%	86%
Dillard University	1,011	97%	73%
Edward Waters College	831	97%	77%
Elizabeth City State University	3,264	94%	66%
Fayetteville State University	6,283	94%	70%
Fisk University	650	93%	54%
Florida A&M University	12,274	96%	58%
Florida Memorial University	1,923	91%	68%
Fort Valley State University	3,553	80%	69%
Gadsden State Community College	6,917	78%	49%
Grambling State University	4,992	96%	68%
Hampton University	5,402	64%	23%
Harris-Stowe State University	1,886	97%	71%

Institute	Total Enrollment (2009–10)	% of Full-time First-time Undergraduates Receiving Financial Aid (2008–09)	% of Full-time First-time Undergraduates Receiving Pell Grants (2008–09)
Hinds Community College-Utica	1,917	N/A	N/A
Howard University	10,573	91%	36%
Huston-Tillotson University	882	94%	72%
Interdenominational Theological Center	421	N/A	N/A
Jackson State University	8,783	89%	72%
Jarvis Christian College	628	87%	68%
J.F. Drake State Technical College	1,258	67%	33%
Johnson C. Smith University	1,466	85%	56%
Kentucky State University	2,834	81%	51%
Knoxville College	100	N/A	N/A
Lane College	2,146	100%	88%
Langston University	2,749	96%	78%
Lawson State Community College-Birmingham Campus	4,353	83%	77%
Le Moyne-Owen College	890	91%	80%
Lewis College of Business	300	N/A	N/A
Lincoln University	3,314	90%	58%
Lincoln University of Pennsylvania	2,649	98%	50%
Livingstone College	1,082	93%	71%
Meharry Medical College	786	N/A	N/A
Miles College	1,791	99%	81%
Mississippi Valley State University	2,850	100%	81%
Morehouse College	2,689	98%	50%

Institute	Total Enrollment (2009–10)	% of Full-time First-time Undergraduates Receiving Financial Aid (2008–09)	% of Full-time First-time Undergraduates Receiving Pell Grants (2008–09)
Morehouse School of Medicine	326	N/A	N/A
Morgan State University	7,226	93%	47%
Morris Brown College	240	N/A	N/A
Morris College	966	98%	84%
Norfolk State University	6,993	91%	52%
North Carolina A&T State University	10,614	92%	56%
North Carolina Central University	8,587	96%	66%
Oakwood University	1,916	92%	33%
Paine College	907	95%	76%
Paul Quinn College	171	90%	76%
Philander Smith College	668	91%	61%
Prairie View A&M University	8,608	94%	66%
Rust College	1,072	82%	77%
Saint Augustine's College	1,529	95%	70%
Saint Paul's College	584	98%	71%
Saint Philip's College	11,008	77%	67%
Savannah State University	3,820	96%	67%
Selma University	35	85%	56%
Shaw University	2,538	98%	72%
Shelton State Community College	5,808	63%	43%
Shorter College	N/A	N/A	N/A
South Carolina State University	4,538	98%	72%
Southern University and A&M College	7,619	97%	66%

Institute	Total Enrollment (2009–10)	% of Full-time First-time Undergraduates Receiving Financial Aid (2008–09)	% of Full-time First-time Undergraduates Receiving Pell Grants (2008–09)
Southern University at New Orleans	3,141	78%	73%
Southern University at Shreveport	3,014	91%	84%
Southwestern Christian College	201	100%	67%
Spelman College	2,229	93%	39%
Stillman College	1,041	93%	82%
Talladega College	700	85%	68%
Tennessee State University	8,824	97%	61%
Texas College	964	100%	99%
Texas Southern University	9,394	95%	72%
Tougaloo College	939	99%	93%
Trenholm State Technical College	1,733	67%	58%
Tuskegee University	2,931	92%	21%
University of Arkansas at Pine Bluff	3,792	76%	72%
University of Maryland Eastern Shore	4,433	99%	53%
University of the District of Columbia	4,960	63%	56%
University of the Virgin Islands	2,602	84%	66%
Virginia State University	5,366	90%	54%
Virginia Union University	1,691	97%	63%
Virginia University of Lynchburg	327	100%	83%
Voorhees College	701	97%	83%
West Virginia State University	4,003	96%	63%

Institute	Total Enrollment (2009–10)	% of Full-time First-time Undergraduates Receiving Financial Aid (2008–09)	% of Full-time First-time Undergraduates Receiving Pell Grants (2008–09)
Wilberforce University	710	100%	72%
Wiley College	1,237	100%	96%
Winston-Salem State University	6,427	94%	60%
Xavier University of Louisiana	3,338	97%	61%

Source: United States Department of Education (2011). Data on Historically Black Colleges and Universities.
Retrieved from http://nces.ed.gov/ipeds/datacenter

HISTORICALLY BLACK COLLEGES AND UNIVERSITIES, ENDOWMENTS AND ALUMNI GIVING

Institute	Total Enrollment (2009–10)	Endowment (2009) (In millions)	Average Alumni Giving Rate
Alabama A&M University	5,327	$119	50%
Alabama State University	5,564	N/A	2%
Albany State University	4,473	N/A	5%
Alcorn State University	3,334	N/A	3%
Allen University	827	$3	5%
Arkansas Baptist College	640	$88	N/A
Barber-Scotia College	N/A	N/A	8%
Benedict College	2,983	$43	27%
Bennett College for Women	766	$10	28%
Bethune-Cookman University	3,637	$39	5%
Bishop State Community College	3,598	N/A	N/A
Bluefield State College	1,989	N/A	17%
Bowie State University	5,617	N/A	8%
Central State University	2,436	N/A	23%

Institute	Total Enrollment (2009–10)	Endowment (2009) (In millions)	Average Alumni Giving Rate
Cheyney University of Pennsylvania	1,488	N/A	6%
Claflin University	1,860	$17	37%
Clark Atlanta University	3,873	$44	10%
Clinton Junior College	148	N/A	N/A
Coahoma Community College	2,565	N/A	N/A
Concordia College-Selma	568	$509,000	N/A
Coppin State University	3,801	N/A	1.3%
Delaware State University	3,609	$20	6%
Denmark Technical College	1,105	N/A	N/A
Dillard University	1,011	$39	5%
Edward Waters College	831	$2	N/A
Elizabeth City State University	3,264	N/A	22%
Fayetteville State University	6,283	$12	4%
Fisk University	650	$13	24%
Florida A&M University	12,274	$88	4%
Florida Memorial University	1,923	$11	N/A
Fort Valley State University	3,553	$12	9%
Gadsden State Community College	6,917	N/A	N/A
Grambling State University	4,992	$119	1%
Hampton University	5,402	$336	14%
Harris-Stowe State University	1,886	N/A	3%
Hinds Community College-Utica	1,917	N/A	N/A
Howard University	10,573	$338	8%
Huston-Tillotson University	882	$7	N/A
Interdenominational Theological Center	421	$12	N/A
Jackson State University	8,783	$12	2.1%
Jarvis Christian College	628	$12	4%
J.F. Drake State Technical College	1,258	N/A	N/A
Johnson C. Smith University	1,466	$51	22%

Institute	Total Enrollment (2009–10)	Endowment (2009) (In millions)	Average Alumni Giving Rate
Kentucky State University	2,834	N/A	3%
Knoxville College	100	$1	N/A
Lane College	2,146	$2	17%
Langston University	2,749	N/A	3%
Lawson State Community College-Birmingham Campus	4,353	N/A	N/A
Le Moyne-Owen College	890	$12	16%
Lewis College of Business	300	N/A	N/A
Lincoln University	3,314	N/A	3.1%
Lincoln University of Pennsylvania	2,649	$23	12%
Livingstone College	1,082	$1	4%
Meharry Medical College	786	N/A	N/A
Miles College	1,791	$14	N/A
Mississippi Valley State University	2,850	N/A	N/A
Morehouse College	2,689	$129	17%
Morehouse School of Medicine	326	N/A	N/A
Morgan State University	7,226	N/A	N/A
Morris Brown College	240	N/A	8%
Morris College	966	$9	42%
Norfolk State University	6,993	N/A	3%
North Carolina A&T State University	10,614	$13	9%
North Carolina Central University	8,587	N/A	10%
Oakwood University	1,916	$6	5%
Paine College	907	$11	9%
Paul Quinn College	171	$7	N/A
Philander Smith College	668	$14	8%
Prairie View A&M University	8,608	$34	6.3%
Rust College	1,072	$24	19%
Saint Augustine's College	1,529	$19	8%
Saint Paul's College	584	$5	6%

Institute	Total Enrollment (2009–10)	Endowment (2009) (In millions)	Average Alumni Giving Rate
Saint Philip's College	11,008	N/A	N/A
Savannah State University	3,820	$2	1%
Selma University	35	N/A	N/A
Shaw University	2,538	$9	5%
Shelton State Community College	5,808	N/A	N/A
Shorter College	N/A	N/A	N/A
South Carolina State University	4,538	N/A	12%
Southern University and A&M College	7,619	$10	3%
Southern University at New Orleans	3,141	N/A	24%
Southern University at Shreveport	3,014	N/A	4%
Southwestern Christian College	201	N/A	N/A
Spelman College	2,229	$352	45%
Stillman College	1,041	$18	5%
Talladega College	700	$5	15%
Tennessee State University	8,824	$28	3%
Texas College	964	$1	N/A
Texas Southern University	9,394	N/A	0.5%
Tougaloo College	939	$8	32%
Trenholm State Technical College	1,733	N/A	N/A
Tuskegee University	2,931	$87	22%
University of Arkansas at Pine Bluff	3,792	N/A	9%
University of Maryland Eastern Shore	4,433	N/A	7.5%
University of the District of Columbia	4,960	$22	0.1%
University of the Virgin Islands	2,602	N/A	6.3%
Virginia State University	5,366	$14	10%
Virginia Union University	1,691	$22	11%
Virginia University of Lynchburg	327	$599,000	N/A
Voorhees College	701	$5	12%
West Virginia State University	4,003	$3	N/A
Wilberforce University	710	$13	N/A

Institute	Total Enrollment (2009–10)	Endowment (2009) (In millions)	Average Alumni Giving Rate
Wiley College	1,237	N/A	39%
Winston-Salem State University	6,427	$20	7.3%
Xavier University of Louisiana	3,338	$133	5%

Sources: National Association of College and University Business Officers (2009). U.S. and Canadian Institutions Listed By Fiscal Year 2009 Endowment Market Value and Percentage Change in Endowment Market Value from FY 2008 to FY 2009. Retrieved from http://www.nacubo.org/Documents/research/2009_NCSE_Public_Tables_Endowment_Market_Values.pdf

Richards, D., & Mann, T. (2011). *UNCF Statistical Report.* Fairfax: Frederick D. Patterson Research institute, UNCF.

United States Department of Education (2011). Data on Historically Black Colleges and Universities. Retrieved from http://nces.ed.gov/ipeds/datacenter

United States Department of Education (2011). List of Historically Black Colleges and Universities. Retrieved from http://www2.ed.gov/about/inits/list/whhbcu/edlite-list.html

U.S. News and World Report (2010). Best Colleges. *U.S. News and World Report,* 40–41.

BIBLIOGRAPHY

Anderson, J. A. (1988). *The education of Blacks in the South, 1865–1930.* Chapel Hill, NC: University of North Carolina Press.

Ashley, D., Gasman, M., Mason, R., Sias, M., and Wright, G. (1999). *Making the grade: Improving degree attainment at historically Black colleges and universities.* New York: Thurgood Marshall College Fund.

Awokoya, J. T. and Mann, T. L. (2011). *Students speak! Understanding the value of HBCUs from student perspectives.* Washington, DC: United Negro College Fund.

Ayers & Associates (2002). *Alumni giving in the new millennium: A guide to securing support.* Washington, DC: Ayers & Associates.

Baade, R. A. and Sundberg, J. O. (1995). What determines alumni generosity? *Economics of Education Review,* 15(1), 75–81.

Barrett, T. G. (2006). How strategic presidential leadership and institutional culture influenced fund-raising effectiveness at Spelman College. *Planning for Higher Education,* October–December, 5–18.

Bowman, N. (2010). Cultivating future fundraisers of color at Historically Black Colleges and Universities. *International Journal of Educational Advancement,* 10(3), 230–234.

Brown, T., Parks, G. S., and Phillips, C. (2010). *African American fraternities and sororities: The legacy and the vision.* Lexington, KY: University of Kentucky Press.

Carter, L. (1998). *Walking integrity: Benjamin E. Mays mentor to Martin Luther King Jr.* Mercer, GA: Mercer University Press.

Chandler, K. W. (2006). The American college president: A study of HBCU and non-HBCU college presidents. Ph.D. Dissertation, University of North Carolina, Greensboro.

Cohen, R. T. (2006). Black college alumni giving: A study of the perceptions, attitudes, and giving behaviors of alumni donors at selected Historically Black Colleges and Universities. Ph.D. Dissertation, Vanderbilt University.

Cohen, R. T. (2008). Alumni to the rescue: Black college alumni and their historical impact on alma mater. *International Journal of Educational Advancement*, 8(1), 25–33.

Cole, J. B. (1994). *Conversations: Straight talk with America's sister president.* New York: Anchor Press.

Cole, J. B. (2003). *Gender talk: The struggle for women's equality in African American communities.* New York: Random House Press.

Coupet, J. and Barnum, D. (2010). HBCU efficiency and endowments: An exploratory analysis. *International Journal of Educational Advancement,* 10(3), 186–197.

Drezner, N. D. (2010). Private Black colleges' encouragement of student giving and volunteerism: An examination of prosocial behavior development. *International Journal of Educational Advancement*, 10(3), 126–147.

Eldredge, R. G. (1999). The advancement president in higher education. Ph.D. Dissertation, Johnson & Wales University.

Fischer, J. L. (1985). Role of the public college or university president in fund raising. In M. J. Worth (ed.), *Public college and university development.* Washington, DC: Council for the Advancement and Support of Education.

Flyin' West Marketing (2011). *Alumni of color.* San Francisco, CA: Flyin' West Marketing.

Freeman, K. and Cohen, R. (2001). Bridging the gap between economic development and cultural empowerment: HBCUs' challenges for the future. *Urban Education*, 36, 585–596.

Gasman, M. (2001). Charles S. Johnson and Johnnetta Cole: Successful role models for fundraising at Historically Black Colleges and Universities. *The CASE International Journal of Educational Advancement*, 1(3), 237–252.

Gasman, M. (2007). *Envisioning Black colleges: A history of the United Negro College Fund.* Baltimore, MD: Johns Hopkins University Press.

Gasman, M. (2010a). A growing tradition? Examining the African American family foundation. *Nonprofit Management & Leadership,* 21(2).

Gasman, M. (2010b). False comparisons: The plight of Historically Black Colleges and Universities. *Chronicle of Higher Education*, www.chronicle.com, accessed July 22, 2011.

Gasman, M. and Anderson-Thompkins, S. (2003). *Fund raising on Black college campuses: Successful strategies for supporting alma mater.* Washington, DC: Council for the Advancement and Support of Education.

Gasman, M., Baez, B., and Turner, C. S. (2008). *Understanding minority serving institutions.* Albany, NY: State University of New York.

Gasman, M. and Sedgwick, K. V. (Eds.) (2005). *Uplifting a people: Essays on African America philanthropy and education.* New York: Peter Laing.

Gasman, M. and Tudico, C. (2008). *Historically Black Colleges and Universities: Triumphs, troubles, and taboos.* New York: Palgrave Press.

Gow-Pettey, J. (2001). *Cultivating diversity in fundraising.* San Francisco, CA: Wiley Books.

Harrison, W. (1994). College relations and fund-raising expenditures: Influencing the probability of alumni giving to higher education. *Economics of Education Review*, 14(1), 73–84.

Harvey, W. R. (2010). Op-ed article to the Wall Street Journal, www.hampton.edu, accessed July 22, 2011.

Hodson, J. B. (2010). Leading the way: The role of presidents and academic deans in fundraising. *New Directions for Higher Education*, 149, 39–49.

Holloman, D., Gasman, M., and Anderson-Thompkins, S. (2003). Motivations for philanthropic giving in the African American church: Implications for Black college fundraising. *Journal of Research on Christian Education*, 12(2), 137–169.

Holmes, J. (2009). Prestige, charitable deductions and other determinants of alumni giving: Evidence from a highly selective liberal arts college. *Economics of Education Review*, 28, 18–28.

Hunter, C. S., Jones, E. B., and Boger, C. (1999). A study of the relationship between alumni giving and selected characteristics of alumni donors of Livingstone College, NC. *Journal of Black Studies*, 29(4), 523–539.

Integrated Postsecondary Educational Database System (2009). Washington, DC: Department of Education.

Jencks, C. and Riesman, D. (1967). The American Negro college. *Harvard Educational Review*, 37(2), 3–60.

Kelderman, E. (2010). Black colleges see a need to improve image. *Chronicle of Higher Education*, www.chronicle.com, accessed July 22, 2011.

Kimbrough, W. (2003). *Black Greek 101: The culture, customs and challenges of*

Black fraternities and sororities. Madison, NJ: Fairleigh Dickenson University Press.

Kimbrough, W. (2007a). The perpetuation of privilege. *Inside Higher Education*, www.insidehighered.com, accessed July 22, 2011.

Kimbrough, W. (June 28, 2007b). In Kamara, M. Are USNEWS rankings inherently biased against African Americans? *Diverse: Issues in Higher Education*, www.diverseeducation.com, accessed July 22, 2011.

Lui, M., Robles, M., and Leondar-Wright, B. (2005). *The color of wealth: The story behind the U.S. racial divide.* New York: New Press.

Malveaux, J. (2009). They don't dislike health care, they dislike Barack Obama. *Chicago Defender*, www.chicagodefender.com, accessed July 22, 2011.

Malveaux, J. (2011). Gender equity is everybody's business. *The Seattle Medium*, www.seattlemedium.com, accessed July 22, 2011.

Masterson, K. (May 10, 2010). Hip hop prez rejuvenates a college using personal touch. *Chronicle of Higher Education*, www.chronicle.com, accessed July 22, 2011.

Mays, B. E. (2003). *Born to rebel: An autobiography.* Athens, GA: University of Georgia Press.

Miree, K. W. (2003). From theory to practice: Three successful models to build endowment. Unpublished Paper, www.kathrynmireeandassociates.com.

National Association of College and University Business Officers (2010). Annual Report. Washington, DC.

National Public Radio (May 3, 2009). Spelman and other colleges cut back. Washington, DC: National Public Radio.

Neuwman, D. (2002). *Opening doors: Pathways to diverse donors.* San Francisco: Jossey-Bass.

Palmer, R. and Gasman, M. (2008). 'It takes a village to raise a child': The role of social capital in promoting academic success for African American men at a Black college. *Journal of College Student Development*, 49(1), 52–70.

Perna, L. W., Lundy-Wagner, V., Drezner, N., Gasman, M., Yoon, S., Bose, E., and Gary, S. (2009). The contribution of HBCUs to the preparation of African American women for STEM careers: A case study. *Research in Higher Education* 50: 1–23.

Pluvoise, D. (2007). Julianne Malveaux named Bennett College President, *Diverse: Issues in Higher Education*, www.diverseeducation.com, accessed July 22, 2011.

Ratliff, B. (2007). Where the game is just a warm up for the band? *The New York Times*, www.nytimes.com, accessed July 22, 2011.

Redden, E. (2009). Reaching Black men. *Inside Higher Education*, www.insidehighered.com, accessed July 22, 2011.

Ross, L. (2001). *The divine nine: The history of African American fraternities and sororities*. New York: Kensington Press.

Rust, A. (2009). *Attaining the dream: How financial resources impact the mission of North Carolina HBCUs*. Raliegh, NC: North Carolina Institute for Minority Economic Development.

Sargeant, A. and Kahler, J. (1999). Returns on fundraising expenditures in the voluntary sector. *Nonprofit Management & Leadership*, 10(1), 5–19.

Schultz, B. S. (2005). *Changing the odds. Lessons learned from the Kresge HBCU Initiative*. Troy, MI: Kresge Foundation.

Smith, B., Shue, S., Vest, J. L., and Villarreal, J. (1999). *Philanthropy in communities of color*. Bloomington, IN: Indiana University Press.

Sorrell, M. (Dec. 28, 2010). Paul Quinn's reality, *Dallas Morning News*.

Sowell, T. ([1930] 1972). *Black education: Myths and tragedies*. New York: McKay.

Stewart, R. (2011). Historically Black schools turning to capital campaigns. *Diverse: Issues in Higher Education*, www.diverseeducation.com, accessed July 22, 2011.

Strayhorn, T. L. (2009). Fittin' In: Do diverse interactions with peers affect sense of belonging for Black men at predominantly White institutions? *The NASPA Journal*, 45(4), 501–527.

Strom, S. (October 27, 2010). Students feel pressured to donate. *The New York Times*, www.nytimes.com, accessed July 22, 2011.

Tatum, B. (1997). *"Why Are All The Black Kids Sitting Together in the Cafeteria?": A Psychologist Explains the Development of Racial Identity*. New York: Basic Books.

Tatum, B. (Feb. 22, 2010). Why Historically Black Colleges and Universities are still relevant, n.p.

Texas Department of State Health Services Center (2006). *Professional nursing education in Texas: Demographics and trends*, 2006. Houston: State of Texas.

Tindall, N. T. J. (2007). Fund-raising models at public Historically Black Colleges and Universities. *Public Relations Review*, 33, 201–255.

Tindall, N. T. J. (2009). Working on the short grass: A qualitative analysis of fundraiser roles and experiences at public Historically Black Colleges and Universities. *International Journal of Educational Advancement*, 9(1), 3–15.

Tindall, N. T. J. (2010). The relationships between fundraising practice and job satisfaction at Historically Black Colleges and Universities. *International Journal of Educational Advancement*, 10(3), 198–215.

United Negro College Fund (2011). *United Negro College Fund Statistical Report*. Washington, DC: Frederick D. Patterson Research Institute.

United States Commission on Civil Rights (2010). *The educational effectiveness of historically Black colleges and Universities*. Washington, DC: U.S. Government.

Walton, A. and Gasman, M. (Eds.). (2008). *Philanthropy, fundraising, and volunteerism in higher education*. Upper Saddle River, NJ: Pearson Publishing.

Weerts, D. J. and Ronca, J. M. (2007). Characteristics of alumni donors who volunteer at their alma mater. *Research in Higher Education*, 49, 274–292.

Whitaker, S. D. (2005). The role of the private college president in fundraising: A comparative case study. Ph.D. Dissertation, University of Louisville.

Willemain, T. R., Goyal, A., Van Deven, M., and Thukral, I. (1994). Alumni giving: The influences of reunion, class, and year. *Research in Higher Education*, 35(5), 609–629.

Williams, M. G. (2010). Increasing philanthropic support through entrepreneurial activities at Historically Black Colleges and Universities, *International Journal of Education Advancement*, 10(3), 216–229.

Williams, M. G. and Kritsonis, W. A. (2006). Raising more money at the nation's historically Black colleges and universities. *National Journal for Publishing and Mentoring Doctoral Student Research*, 3(1), 1–6.

Williamson, J. A. (2008). *Radicalizing the ebony tower: Black colleges and the Black freedom struggle in Mississippi*. New York: Teachers College Press.

Wilson, J. S. (2010). America's Historically Black Colleges and Universities and the third transformation. *The Presidency*, 16–17.

Wunnava, P. V. and Lauze, M. A. (2000). Alumni giving at a small liberal arts college: Evidence from consistent and occasional donors. *Economics of Education Review*, 20, 533–543.

INDEX